Ashchurch
for Tewkesbury

8745

es & West

RAILWAY LIVERIES:
Privatisation 1995-2000

RAILWAY LIVERIES:
Privatisation 1995-2000

Colin Boocock

Ian Allan
PUBLISHING

ACKNOWLEDGEMENTS

The author is indebted to the following who helped the production of this book by supplying information or diagrams: Richard Bourne (GNER), Alison Brown (Freightliner), Alan Braithwaite (Silverlink), Andy Lickfold (EWS), John Morris (Wales & West), Ian Ross (First Great Eastern), Joanna Smyth (First Great Western), Ray Stenning (Best Impressions), Dave Taylor (EWS), Don Townsley (Mott MacDonald), Rob Walker (Virgin Trains) and Mark Wilcox (First North Western). Their help has enabled this book to become a definitive record of train liveries after privatisation.

Photographs

All photographs were taken by the author, Colin Boocock, unless otherwise credited. I happily acknowledge the assistance of the railway photographers who diligently searched their recent collections for specific illustrations, namely Hugh Ballantyne, Tony Miles, Colin J. Marsden, Brian Morrison, John Stretton and Bob Sweet. Without them the picture would be far less complete, if total completeness is ever possible.

First published 2001

ISBN 0 7110 2783 8

All rights reserved. No part of this book may be reproduced or transmitted in any form or by any means, electronic or mechanical, including photocopying, recording or by any information storage and retrieval system, without permission from the Publisher in writing.

© Colin Boocock 2001

Published by Ian Allan Publishing

an imprint of Ian Allan Publishing Ltd, Hersham, Surrey KT12 4RG.
Printed by Ian Allan Printing Ltd, Hersham, Surrey KT12 4RG.

Code: 0107/B3

All photographs were taken by the author, unless otherwise

Title page:
Modernity is the theme for many new train liveries, which often make use of the streamlining effect of dark ribbon glazing of carriages. Anglia Railways' Class 170 DMUs are a case in point. These use vinyl strips to enable more complex rendering of colours. Unit 170 201 was heading the 14.40 to London Liverpool Street at Norwich on 9 September 1999.

Main title page:
HSTs in the new GNER livery of midnight blue with red stripe soon gained the nickname 'stealth bombers' because of their sharp frontal appearance. This unit is passing Finsbury Park on 10 April 2000 near the end of its journey on the 09.55 service from Aberdeen to London King's Cross. Note that the red line is terminated before it reaches the radiator panel on the power car.

Right:
The smart colours of Thameslink trains attract travellers to these useful services. Unit 319 456 rushes through South Croydon on 13 May 1999 working the 13.12 from Bedford to Brighton.

Back cover (upper):
Anglia Railways applied shaded acetates as part of the new livery used for their Adtranz-built Class 170 DMUs. The turquoise was that used in painted version of the livery on older stock. Note the different treatment of the passenger entrance doors to comply with the requirements for partially-sighted people.

Back cover (lower):
English, Welsh & Scottish Railway developed its locomotive liveries entirely in-house without the use of consultants. The result is generally regarded as pleasing, an adaptation of the colours used on the parent company's locomotives in the USA. No 66144 stands at Toton depot in EWS maroon on 10 May 2000.

Front cover (main):
Thameslink adopted a boldly-coloured livery to replace the unpopular all-over grey that had been applied to the trains in the last year of BR ownership of the train operating company. Unit 319 443 approaches South Croydon on 13 May 1999 on the 12.57 from Bedford to Brighton.

Front cover (inset top):
Great Western changed their livery after being taken over by First Group by the simple application of shaded acetates to the lower bodyside panels. This change uses stripes of progressively varying thicknesses to form visual fading, leading the eye to the gold band in which is inserted the brand name. This is the version applied to High Speed Train carriages.

Front cover (inset upper):
Bright colour contrasts resulted from Connex applying yellow shaded acetates to the lower bodysides on Networker EMUs, which retained the NSE blue upper panels because they were not due for repainting. Other units received white upper panels were repainted.

Front cover (inset lower):
This short-lived variation of the Virgin logo includes reference to the CrossCountry allocation of the HST fleet. Later trains all have just the plain Virgin symbol, whether belonging to WestCoast or CrossCountry.

Front cover (inset bottom):
Northern Spirit used light blue as the main body colour for its general purpose DMUs, with the company logo (the big 'N'), applied in lime green.

CONTENTS

INTRODUCTION

What Are Train Liveries For?

For a century and a half, railways have painted trains to prevent deterioration of the metal, wood or other material from which they are made. There have been some exceptions, notably those trains made of 'inoxidisable' metals such as stainless steel or aluminium. Some railway administrations made use of the indestructible property of stainless metals to reduce their painting costs. This action was regarded as 'modern' in some quarters, certainly in the 1950s and 1960s, when the sight of 'silver' trains was seen to be an advance on the dull appearance of many painted trains of earlier years. London Underground, and SNCF in France, operate some unpainted trains, as still do the railways of Portugal, though in these administrations this is changing fast as the trend towards brighter colours takes hold.

Modern train operators want their customers and potential customers to be attracted to train travel by the outward appearance of their trains. They want fast trains to look sleek and speedy. Suburban trains in conurbations need to please their local authority paymasters, who have a right to expect their local trains to look smart. Train operators in Britain now have to make life easier for visually-challenged passengers by painting entrance doors in contrasting colours. Others hope that their train liveries exude an aura of quality and service. All want to look different from their neighbours.

Above left:
Class 47 Co-Co No 47817 in Porterbrook Leasing purple and white livery deputises for a Virgin CrossCountry locomotive at the head of the 10.44 from Plymouth to Manchester, at Eckington Bridge on 12 December 1997. Such unusual mixtures of colours can occur from time to time as privatised operators hire locomotives or stock from each other to make up occasional shortages. *Bob Sweet*

Left:
GNER's strong image comes from use of a simple livery of midnight blue, said to be inherited from Sea Containers' VSOE trains on the continent, set off with a light red stripe along the bodysides. The singular Brush Co-Co electric locomotive No 89001 in this view of the 10.05 to London King's Cross taken at Leeds on 12 August 1998 had the interim white-coloured GNER decals; the final decision for these was 'retro-reflective' gold. *Tony Miles*

Privatisation

The prospect of British Rail (BR) being split up into 25 Train Operating Companies and two or three freight companies excited students of railway train liveries. After all, the quickest way for a new company to identify itself with the general public as being different from its neighbours is to change its corporate image, and this includes re-packaging its product. In the context of railways, this means changing the colours it paints its trains, as well as station signing, publicity material, letterheads and indeed everything that the public sees as being part of the image of that company.

The letting of passenger railway franchises to private companies took place from the middle of 1995 to early 1997. This author expresses his surprise that not all train operators were quick off the mark in this pursuit of sartorial splendour for their trains. Faced with an opportunity to display their image and thus show the travelling public that they were in business, only a few began to paint their trains irrespective of whether painting was due. Gatwick Express, one of the very first to be privatised, economically modified the former BR InterCity colours on its locomotives and stock, and so was able to look different early on. Great North Eastern Railway (GNER) repainted its trains in its dark blue colours within a couple of years. National Express, owner of Midland Mainline, was similarly speedy in splashing out on green with tangerine stripes, tied to the already-planned refurbishment of its High Speed Trains (HSTs). On the suburban front, the Thameslink company was clearly in a hurry to rid itself of the radical grey livery that BR's nascent Train Operating Unit had thought the franchisee would like, and Stagecoach took only a little longer to apply new colours to trains using Waterloo. LTS, on the other hand, played safe, with a replacement of part of the NSE lining on its trains to change their image without great expense — quite effectively, as it turned out.

At the opposite end of the image-change race, Thames Trains and Cardiff Railways were among the last in coming up with new liveries, and Wales & West has only just dipped its brush in the paint pot, so to speak.

Most surprising was the apparently slow pace at which Virgin Trains managed to get its (admittedly) striking colours onto its trains. What everyone

expected was that Virgin's policy for putting customers first, coupled with its flair for publicity, would manifest itself in quickly splashing the company's colours across the network. Instead, Virgin has apparently been satisfied with re-liverying only when trains become due for overhaul, just like BR did before it. Thus at the time of writing there are still Virgin West Coast locomotives and some Cross Country trains running around in former BR InterCity colours (and a few still so labelled), some of which are quite disreputable in appearance as paint wears out and filler flakes off. This situation provides a good illustration of the need to plan train-painting cycles to match the expected ability of paint systems to maintain their protective and decorative surfaces.

Freight companies tend to operate at the practical end of the railway-management spectrum rather than the emotional, and so the new liveries for their locomotives and wagons have tended to spread more slowly across the network. Nonetheless, there are some gems that are described in this book.

Changing Styles

The battle for passenger business has produced some surprisingly short-term image changes. Some companies have had second thoughts on train

Above:
The Virgin symbol was first intended also to indicate to which franchise a service belonged. This HST power car with its 'XC' embellishment showed its allegiance to the CrossCountry franchise. All Virgin trains now just carry the name of the holding company, Virgin.

Above right:
The plum colour of Northern Spirit's Trans-Pennine Express Class 158 units changes according to the angle and intensity of light, as does the reflective gold 'Big N' symbol. This highly distinctive livery uses form rather than colour as the brand mark of Northern Spirit. Unit 158 798 was photographed at Leeds on 11 March 1999.

Right:
Mk 2 locomotive-hauled stock in the First Great Western fleet was painted in the new FirstGroup style when first re-liveried. Note that, as on the HST carriages, the vehicle ends are black and all handrails are white. Step-boards are yellow. Note also that the British Standard (as opposed to railway standard) yellow triangle 'overhead live wire' plate is applied on the vehicle ends just below the gutter. The gutters are painted orange, thus forming the OHLE warning line. *Colin J. Marsden*

liveries early in their franchise periods. For example, while South West Trains adapted the style of the former BR Network SouthEast for its suburban trains, but with colour shades that emulated

Stagecoach's buses, the company went very bold when considering the repainting of its flagship electric multiple-units (EMUs) — the Class 442 sets that operate to Bournemouth and Portsmouth. Great Western Trains, too, had only just announced that all its fleet of HSTs was now in green and ivory when a new style emerged with a striking variation of the colour scheme.

Companies such as Gatwick Express, First Great Western, First North Western and Anglia have changed their style completely when taking delivery of new trains, which now present a different image again from the existing trains that they repainted in their original corporate colours. Chapter 7 chronicles these later developments.

Overlaps From The Past

This book describes the train liveries introduced by the private companies that emerged from the privatisation of British Rail. A number of liveries that come from an earlier era are still visible on the Railtrack network. Former BR colours that survive are described in the author's book *Railway Liveries: BR Traction 1948-1995* (Ian Allan Publishing, 2000), which also includes the liveries of the Passenger Transport Executives (PTEs) which support trains operating in our major conurbations. The PTE liveries have continued generally

Above:
First Great Eastern Class 321 EMU No 321 317 calls at Shenfield on a London Liverpool Street-Southminster service on 31 July 1998. The green, grey and blue stripes in the livery change have been achieved entirely using vinyl sheets, leaving intact some of the NSE grey area and the blue window band. Note the small FirstGroup insignia above the centre coupling, and that the painted NSE blue across the window band is not the same shade as the decal Great Eastern blue lining.

unchanged into the privatisation era, with two exceptions at the time of writing (early 2001). The unchanged PTE liveries are not described again in this book.

The book also does not cover those many private-sector freight companies that had shunting locomotives or wagons operating on BR tracks before privatisation, although the popular aggregates operations using Class 59 locomotives are covered briefly for completeness. Also excluded are heritage liveries used by some independent suppliers of motive power and carriages, since these liveries have already been described in earlier books.

This book illustrates key examples of liveries chosen by the companies that operate on-track machinery for track and infrastructure inspection and maintenance.

Paint Systems

Technology moves on. Even the relatively humble task of painting trains has become much more scientific in recent years. Very high-gloss finishes with a potential life of over 10 years are now possible. These use what are described as 'two-pack' paints, applied by spray. Painters and other personnel in the vicinity of the painting and drying have to be specially protected from the fumes that are given off as solvents dissolve and chemicals cure. Among the first trains to use two-pack paints were NSE's Class 465 EMUs. The technique leaves a very hard and impenetrable surface that is not easily damaged. Hence many recently-constructed trains have had body shells delivered fully-painted from one factory (often an overseas one), ready for mounting on bogies and fitting-out at another.

The act of rubbing down a two-pack-painted unit for a livery change releases potentially harmful powder that is costly to contain and extract during preparations for a repaint. This appears to have made some operating companies wary of embarking on early livery changes, and explains why, on its Class 465s, Connex South Eastern made extensive use of plastic decals to add a different colour to adapt the former NSE livery to something closer to its house style. It is probably why both Thames Trains and Chiltern Railways initially adopted a no-change policy with the liveries of their Class 165 and 166 DMUs. Modern vinyl, adhesive sheets appear to be able to resist physical and chemical attacks from carriage-washing plants better than did earlier decals. Their only visual disadvantage to date has been in controlling colour rendering, and thus there are sometimes slight variations of the livery colours on adjacent decal strips. One manufacturer guarantees its vinyls for up to eight years' life in a train-livery application.

The availability of firmly-adhering decals has enabled the development, popular on continental railways, of temporary advertising liveries with, in some cases, very complex imagery, and British operators are making increasing use of this system. An early and notable adventure was the Eurostar train that was reliveried for a re-launch of The Beatles' *Yellow Submarine* film in 1999.

With the relative permanence of two-pack paint systems militating against easy repainting of trains, one can expect there to be much more use of plastic film for livery changes in the future.

Below:
Some vinyl decals applied to Connex trains have not been successful in matching pigment intensity in different batches. On this Class 421 unit the join shows up clearly! Notice also the deliberate visual fading of the yellow colour towards the left end of the decal.

76100

1. HIGH SPEED AND INTERCITY TRAINS

When the privatisation of BR was underway there was a movement for co-operation in marketing among those companies that operated what were previously known as InterCity trains. The idea was that joint promotion of timetables, ticketing and fares offers, for example, would benefit the whole market. The name 'InterCity' had achieved widespread brand recognition among residents in the UK, and there was a reluctance to lose this. Had this approach prevailed, the much-admired livery of BR's InterCity trains might well have survived for some time in the privatisation era.

It was not to be. Gatwick Express broke away very quickly from the rest, in 1994, and Virgin Trains was clearly going to attempt to cash in on its own worldwide image as a popular transatlantic carrier and customer-friendly company. GNER, meanwhile, wanted to focus on its own brand of quality product, and other companies also chose to abandon any thought of continuing with the InterCity brand name. Great Western Trains, however, believed that there would be kudos in being the only rail company in Britain to advertise its services as 'InterCity', registering the name and applying it to its trains. Passengers, however, soon understood that they were travelling not so much by InterCity as by Great Western, and the name was eventually dropped,

Above left:
With the advent of adhesive vinyl sheet, advertising liveries have become far more economic to apply and remove. This Eurostar train was 'decorated' with images promoting the re-release of The Beatles' film *Yellow Submarine*. Eurostar units 3005 and 3006 pass Wandsworth Road station with the 11.57 London Waterloo to Paris Nord on 8 September 1999. The livery remained in place for about three months. *Brian Morrison*

Left:
Looking not too different from a former British Rail InterCity train, Gatwick Express Class 73/2 Bo-Bo electro-diesel No 73205 approaches South Croydon on 13 May 1999 with the 13.45 from London Victoria to Gatwick Airport. The upper parts of the train carry the same colours as those used by InterCity, particularly the dark falcon grey. The dark red lining band is lower than the InterCity red band used to be, and of course the logo is specific to the train operator. The locomotive number is placed low on the left cabside.

though not until most GWT HSTs had been so branded.

Gatwick Express

Gatwick Express at once wanted to change its image while keeping the overall InterCity look of its stock — after all, Gatwick Express was the only frequent InterCity presence south of London on the Brighton line, in an area thick with outer-suburban stock. The upper body panels retained their falcon grey colour. Below the windows was a single, dark red lining band, below which the bodyside was off-white. A new 'GATWICK EXPRESS' logo was applied in white to the dark grey area on the locomotive sides, and in dark grey to the light colour below the side windows on the carriages. The locomotive fronts remained warning yellow with falcon-grey window surrounds. Locomotive and carriage running-numbers were affixed in rail alphabet — white on dark grey, and dark grey on off-white.

On the driving vans (GLVs) the cab fronts had the window area above the warning panel painted falcon grey, but, above the overhead line electrification (OHLE) orange warning line, the cab fronts were black — the same as the roof colour.

Great North Eastern Railway

The InterCity East Coast franchise was awarded to Sea Containers Ltd, which adopted the name 'Great North Eastern Railway' (GNER). Sea Containers' other well-known railway enterprise is the Venice-Simplon Orient Express (VSOE), whose continental train is decked out in the deep blue colour used by the former Wagon Lits company. A similar blue was selected for GNER trains, in the hope that the quality image of the VSOE would transfer to GNER. (In retrospect this has been a successful move, as GNER has thus far delivered a quality customer product which is second to none in the UK.)

Early Start

Sea Containers Ltd had already decided on the basic layout of its train livery before it received confirmation of the East Coast Main Line franchise. The New York firm of stylists, Vignelli, had been given the VSOE midnight blue colour and a few basic requirements, and came up with the

simple livery we all now like. A Mk 4 coach had been liveried by Railcare at Babcock Rosyth, originally with differing types of paint surface finish, and with all bodyside passenger information applied to the red band. The only significant change for volume application to the style on this prototype vehicle was the placing of items such as seat numbers and coach identification letters on the upper bodysides, alongside the access doorways.

GNER trains are thus painted overall midnight blue (Pantone 5395), relieved only by a broad red band (Pantone 032) below the bodyside windows, continued onto the bodysides at the 'blunt' end of each power car, locomotive or driving trailer. The OHLE warning line is also applied in red — a livery concession from Railtrack which is no longer granted. Cab roofs and vehicle roofs are also blue. The yellow warning panel is restricted to the area below the cab windscreens, its dimensions limited so that it is forward-facing only. The resultant effect is powerful, and the frontal aspect of the HST power cars in particular has given rise to the nickname 'stealth bombers' among the railway enthusiast fraternity.

The GNER logo is applied in large, gold lettering in Futura font (Light for the 'G' and 'R' letters and Extra Bold for the '**NE**') to the lower bodysides on power cars and locomotives. Some powered vehicles had this logo applied in white for a short period in 1999 when the underlying blue was found to show through the original gold decals. However, gold was still preferred, and all vehicles have reverted to it in an opaque but 'retro-reflective' form. Locomotive and power car numbers are set in light sans serif in blue within the red band, towards the 'blunt' end. (I cannot use my preferred term, 'non-driving' end, because of the small driving cab at the back of a Class 91 locomotive.)

On carriages, the vehicle number is also applied in the red band. A powerful marketing tool is the application in mid-bodyside below the windows of a cast brass GNER badge in traditional railway style (on all HSTs and six of the IC225 sets; the remaining Mk 4s have the badge attached as a vinyl on grounds of cost, but are visually just as effective). Above this is the inspired message 'ROUTE OF THE FLYING SCOTSMAN', applied discreetly in small white sans-serif capitals. Below the bodysides everything is black. On First-class carriages the inscription 'FIRST CLASS' is placed in light Futura font in white on the red band beside the entrance doors. The formerly-standard yellow band above the windows to denote First class was abandoned, as was the red band for catering cars. The overall effect of the livery of a GNER train is of a distinctive, quality product that is modern, yet wisely builds on its successful heritage.

Left:
'Retro-reflective' gold decals enable the GNER logo to shine out in certain lighting conditions. These two Class 91 Bo-Bo electric locomotives were at rest at Newcastle station on 28 July 1999.

Above:
For a period in 1999 the GNER symbol was applied in white to a number of locomotives, after the underlying blue colour was found to show through the original gold. The final version is 'retro-reflective' gold applied as Scotchcal decals. No 91018 was seen with white decals at Doncaster on 18 June 1998 with the 10.30 London King's Cross-Edinburgh.

Below:
'Route of the Flying Scotsman', a brilliant marketing stroke that identifies GNER trains with the East Coast route. The badge beneath is actually a decal on this Mk 4 coach, though on six rakes of Mk 4s and on all GNER's HSTs the badges are brass castings. Note that the overhead line electrification (OHLE) warning line in this application is red to match the GNER red stripe on the carriages — a dispensation from Railtrack in view of the closeness of GNER red to the standard orange. The metal window frames are fully painted-over in this livery.

ROUTE OF THE FLYING SCOTSMAN

Classic Badges

The GNER badges were also designed by Vignelli following a brief education in Britain's traditional railway heraldry. The final design was approved by the College of Arms and the Lord Lyon's office, but has not been registered as an heraldic device, which is why GNER always refers to it as a badge rather than a crest.

From 2000 three Eurostar sets (from the apparently unwanted North-of-London group of seven) were leased to Great North Eastern Railway to enable more frequent services to be timetabled on the East Coast main line. Used on services from London King's Cross that terminated at York, two of the trains were reliveried using all-over blue vinyls printed in the standard GNER colours. Because of the positioning of the bodyside grilles on the power cars and outer-end passenger vehicles, the red line stops at the end of the passenger accommodation. The red line is positioned just below the bodyside windows, respecting the design of the train, even though this means its height above rail level differs from that on the earlier GNER trains. Looking at the borrowed Eurostars, one would never know that they had not been painted in full GNER style.

Locomotive Names

The practice of naming locomotives resumed under GNER following a brief period when nameplates had been removed to enable the corporate GNER style to gain recognition. On the Class 91 electric Bo-Bos the names are applied in 'retro-reflective' gold lettering, on the blue area in front of and in line with the end of the red lining band.

Great Western Trains

There were those observers who hoped that the franchisee, following its adoption of the name 'Great Western', would turn the clock back and apply the former GWR chocolate and cream livery to its trains. Indeed, one well-known railway modeller

Below:
GNER eschewed nameplates on its locomotives and power cars, preferring to attach gold decals as shown here. The name *Peterborough Cathedral* on Class 91 Bo-Bo No 91028 is applied in 'retro-reflective' gold Futura Extra Bold lettering, the top of the capitals being lined up with the top of the GNER logo and the top of the red lining band. This locomotive was photographed at Doncaster on 9 March 2000.

painted up a model to demonstrate how handsome an HST would look in these colours. Great Western Trains (GWT) had other ideas: its chosen colours were silver-white and olive green, applied to HSTs in the modern style with the dark colour along the window area and the white above and below; a narrow band of ivory ran along the base of the bodysides. Small yellow warning panels were applied below the cab windscreens, and vehicle roofs were black. Bodyside window frame beadings were left unpainted.

A new logo was commissioned which was applied in either silver-white or green, in opposition to the background colour. The logo was an elliptical shape and contained a stylised merlin which faced the driving end on HST power cars, otherwise always facing left. The name 'Great Western' was applied to the lower bodysides on carriages at the left end, with the former 'INTERCITY' lettering at the right-hand end, with the 'registered' symbol '®' adjacent. When the InterCity idea began to pale as a marketing tool, the term 'Great Western' was applied instead, thus appearing on both ends of the carriage bodysides. First-class coaches were identified by the formerly-standard yellow band at cantrail level, but the corresponding red band that BR used to apply to catering cars was omitted.

In 1999, recognising its newly-acquired ownership by FirstGroup, GWT introduced a revised livery style using the same colours but employing vinyl decals. These are applied to the lower bodysides of the HSTs, on top of the existing green and ivory livery. The decal has a silver-white base and carries a central gold stripe that is surrounded by a series of parallel green lines that become thicker as they near the edge of the decal. The effect from a normal viewing distance is to fade the lighter colour into the dark green of the upper bodysides and down to the bottom edge of the body. A revision to the cab-front livery replaces the silver-grey at the base of the cab front with a dark green area, also using decals.

The FirstGroup logo in gold is placed well forward on the upper sides of HST power cars. In a

Below:
An HST in the original Great Western Trains livery approaches Reading on 12 April 1999 while working the 13.15 from London Paddington to Bristol Temple Meads. This set is one that has the term 'Great Western' applied at both ends of the lower bodysides. Note also the thin white line between the yellow and the dark green. The GWT 'merlin' emblem in green on a silver-white background is placed on the green band on the power car side, centrally above 'Great Western'.

Above left:
This close-up of the Great Western Trains livery shows a car with the former BR term *'INTERCITY'* at the left end of the lower bodyside. Note the registered mark '®' against the *'INTERCITY'*. GWT soon stopped using this former BR marketing name in favour of just *'Great Western'*. GWT was one of the few train operators to continue to use the popular yellow stripe to denote the position in the train of the First-class sections. Additionally, large '1' figures in white were placed alongside the First-class entrance doors. Coach letters were in white lower-case rail alphabet. The frames of the carriage windows were left unpainted.

Left:
The Great Western Trains 'merlin' symbol was graceful, applied in green on silver-white.

Above:
The first version of the GWT livery for locomotives is seen on Class 47 Co-Co No 47813 after arrival at London Waterloo on 13 June 1998 with the previous evening's 22.00 sleeping-car train from Penzance. The locomotive is in overall dark green with a black roof, white 'merlin' logo and *'Great Western'* underneath. The cab front is also green, with the lower half forming the warning-yellow panel. Its nameplate *SS Great Britain* is in the former BR style, with raised letters cast integrally with the aluminium nameplate, in this case painted with a black background. The 25mm-deep orange OHLE warning line is prominent below the roof line. At this time the locomotive-hauled stock had not been re-liveried from its BR InterCity colours.

smaller size the logo also appears in dark green halfway along the gold band on each carriage. This is accompanied at a distance by gold '**Great Western**' lettering placed on a length of the gold band that has been faded into dark green. The First-class yellow band is still there below the cantrail, but the figure '1' by each entrance door to First-class accommodation is gold instead of the previous white. The carriage-designation letters, which were formerly lower-case in white, are now upper-case in gold. The former GWT merlin logo is no more. No painting was involved in this livery change.

The Class 47 locomotives used for hauling GWT passenger trains were painted dark green overall with standard warning yellow treatment for the cabs. The 'merlin' emblem and *'Great Western'* script were applied towards one end of the bodyside, and locomotive numbers low-down on the bodyside, behind the cabside driver's door, in white rail alphabet. Later, the 1999 gold band was added to the bodysides at about the same height as on the HST vehicles, and the FirstGroup logo replaced the merlin. FGW locomotive-hauled Mk 2 carriages are painted in a similar style to the Mk 3 coaches in the HSTs. Car-carrying vans are painted overall green, with the gold band placed as on the HST vehicles.

Top:
After being taken over by FirstGroup, Great Western adapted its livery by the simple application of shaded acetates to the lower bodyside panels on all stock and the addition of the FirstGroup '*f*' logo on the upper part of power cars, as seen on this HST at Cardiff on 9 February 2000. This change uses stripes of progressively varied thickness to form visual fading, leading the eye to the gold band in which is inserted the power car number. The Great Western name no longer appears on HST power cars. This livery modification was achieved without repainting!

Above:
On First Great Western HST trailer cars the FirstGroup '*f*' symbol appears in the centre of the gold band, flanked at a distance on both sides by the name '**Great Western**' in gold on a part of the band that is faded out to dark green. This re-branded train has the coach letters in gold upper-case.

Top:
The modified livery on Class 47 locomotives added the gold band and replaced the 'merlin' symbol and other branding with the FirstGroup logo. '**Great Western**' appeared near the right end of the gold band, not directly under the FirstGroup logo, and at the opposite end from the locomotive number (in this case 47815). As on carriages, the FirstGroup '*f*' symbol appears in the middle of the gold band in dark green. The nameplate (*Abertawe Landore*) is still in BR-style lettering with a black background.
Colin J. Marsden

Above:
First Great Western Motorail vans, rebuilt from Mk 1 vehicles, are painted all-over dark green with the gold band in place at the now-standard height above rail level but with no shaded decals. The side-door wooden bars are painted orange. The term '**Motorail**' appears in white sans-serif lettering at each end of each van, lined up centrally with the orange door-bars. *Colin J. Marsden*

HST power car No 43074, photographed at Sheffield on 26 April 1999, illustrates perfectly most features of the Midland Mainline livery. In particular note the sweep of the tangerine bands upwards from the corner of the cab front, spreading out to form the parallel lines along the train that contrast so well with the 'teal' green. The lower bodysides and cab-front base are silver-gleam, separated from the green by a thin white line. Note also the sympathetic sweep up of the yellow area of the cab front. The 'leaping stag' motif and company branding in bold white capitals edged in black can be seen clearly. The initial 'M' letters are very slightly larger than the rest. The back feet of the stag fit in a small break in the tangerine lines.

Power car No 43060 at the rear of a Sheffield-bound train at London St Pancras station illustrates the shape of the warning-yellow area, and also shows how the silver-gleam paint runs below the green at the bottom of the cab front. Note that the orange OHLE warning line continues level all round the train, except along the upper ventilation grilles, which are black. Grab-rails are white.

A different treatment is used for the new MML Class 170 DMUs. The tangerine lines are closer together and lower on the bodyside. The 'leaping stag' spreads over a passenger side window, and the smaller, carriage-style Midland Mainline branding is used, above the end passenger windows. The obstacle-deflector is black. Unit 170 102 was photographed when exhibited new at the Railtech '98 exhibition in Birmingham on 24 October 1998.

Midland Mainline

One of four franchises to be gained by National Express, Midland Mainline was quick off the mark with its new livery, taking advantage of the timely start of the refurbishing programme already set up for its fleet of 13 HSTs by BR. The scheme, devised by an image consultant, was initially regarded as unconventional and was accorded an accolade in one of the railway magazines, which stated that this was the most appropriate treatment of the HST power car front end of all the liveries yet applied.

The base bodyside colour is a mid-green biased towards the blue end of the spectrum and known in railway circles (only) as 'teal green'. This is applied over each whole carriage bodyside up to the roof-edge weld line above cantrail level, apart from a beige band (officially 'silver gleam') along the bodyside bottom edge, and is in matching position on the power cars. Bodyside window frames are painted teal green, with no bare beading. Three 65mm-wide tangerine lines are spaced between the bodyside windows and the beige band. The orange OHLE warning line is in the usual position above the windows, and co-ordinates well with the tangerine lining below. There is a 25mm white line edging the beige band. Carriage ends and roofs are black, as are underframe farings and bogies.

Above:
**This view of two Class 170s at St Pancras on 12 April 1999
illustrates the different proportions of the Midland
Mainline livery compared with HST carriages (right). Note
the pale green upper parts of the Class 170 passenger
access doors, to aid the visually-challenged. On the HST
carriages the metal window frames are painted-over.**

The power cars feature a splendid sweep of the combined teal green, tangerine and silver gleam bands upwards from below the lamp clusters. The green is also brought over the cab doors, finishing well above cantrail level. The area of warning yellow on the cab front has been reduced (compared with the former InterCity livery) by not going below the pointed edge of the cab front below the lamp clusters, and by an extension of the roof black forward to about 500mm above the cab windscreen, but is extended further round the cabsides almost to embrace the cab corner windows. The silver gleam band runs across the bottom of the cab front.

When clean, the frontal aspect of a Midland Mainline HST is impressive, but perhaps the railway needs to regularise cleaning at times when train sets are at a non-electrified depot (such as Derby), so that the front view can always be maintained in its intended, striking form. Indeed, keeping the yellow front acceptably clean proved a long-term difficulty for several of the BR Regions, and has done so for other train operators running HSTs.

A striking feature of the Midland Mainline livery is the application on the power car sides of the company logo in the form of a white-outlined leaping stag, ahead of the company name in white block serif lettering. On the HST power car sides, behind the emblem, the words '**MIDLAND MAINLINE**' are placed high on the bodysides behind the cab doors. On Mk 3 coaches the Midland Mainline name appears at one end of the upper bodyside beside the entrance door and just below cantrail level.

For its new Class 170 DMUs, Midland Mainline adapted the HST livery to fit around the black 'ribbon glazing' of the 'Turbostar' bodysides by reducing the area of the teal green and the width and spacing of the three tangerine lines. The cab front had the standard Adtranz placement of the warning yellow just above and below the windscreen, with the bodyside teal green carried right round.

There is no obvious room for the full-size 'leaping stag' logo on Class 170 bodysides, and an unusual treatment is applied, with the stag image splashed across the lower bodyside behind the cab door but also encroaching on a passenger window. The '**MIDLAND MAINLINE**' lettering is set in smaller letters on the green above the windows at each end of a two-car unit. Also on the 'Turbostars', the passenger access doors are painted a very pale shade of green

Above:
Midland Mainline painted its diesel shunting locomotive, No 08899, in 'teal' green and tangerine to work the carriage depot at Derby Etches Park. Features to note are the cramped layout of the full-size 'MIDLAND MAINLINE' lettering against the smaller stag used on the '170' DMUs, the locomotive number spaced out as once *de rigeur* on BR (as 08 899), the unexplained Union Jack below the cabside number, and the red buffer-beam. Orange coupling rods and cab steps, and white-rimmed wheels and buffers finish it off well. In the left background is blue-liveried No 08690, which belongs to Maintrain, the train-maintenance branch of National Express. This one has red coupling rods.
Brian Morrison

above the orange lines, to assist access by partially-sighted people.

On all Midland Mainline trains, the vehicle numbers are in black, placed below the windows, at the right-hand end of the bodysides of HST coaches, on the silver gleam area behind the cab doors of HST power cars (in 200mm capital-height Stone Sans typeface on power cars only), and under the bodyside windows at the inner ends of the two-car '170' units. 'Turbostar' set numbers are on the warning-yellow area, below the driver's side windscreen.

On none of the Midland Mainline trains is any effort made specifically to point out the location of First-class and catering vehicles, other than by large

figures '1' by the appropriate entrance doors; the former yellow and red bands have been discarded.

Midland Mainline Nameplates
This company paints its nameplates with black backgrounds, and uses heavier lettering with serifs.

Virgin Trains
Everyone expected Richard Branson's Virgin company to invent something remarkable for its train livery, and indeed it did! Red is the dominant colour, applied to all vehicle bodysides. The roofs and about 4m of the bodysides at each end are painted very dark grey — the same shade as the former InterCity falcon grey — raked off at a near-vertical angle. The red area below the side windows sports three parallel white lines which just extend into the dark grey area. Diesel and electric locomotives are similarly liveried. HST power cars and West Coast main line driving van trailers (DVTs) are also red, with the red taken to the front of the bodysides, but the non-driving ends have a longer expanse of falcon grey that carries the three short, white lining bands. Cab fronts are warning yellow on HSTs but with the raked back bottom face painted red. On DVTs, the cab-front edges are white with a similarly-constrained yellow panel. Cab roofs are black, and on

Left:

A newly-painted train of Virgin West Coast Mk 3 stock approaches Crewe station on 15 May 1999 while working the 14.45 service from Liverpool Lime Street to London Euston. Note that the white lining on the driving van trailer (DVT) is wholly on the dark grey (looks like black!) area of the bodyside, and that the cab front has white vertical columns at the sides. The Virgin logo on the DVT is applied virtually full-body-height in the red area next to the dark grey. The First-class coaches at the front of this train have yellow bands across the top of the dark grey sections.

Below left:

This treatment of Virgin CrossCountry HST trailer cars follows exactly the same standard as the West Coast trains. On carriages the Virgin logo is always smaller and placed near the passenger entrance doors, low on the dark grey area. Note the small red-backed decals carrying the coach identification letters, just below the central door-locking/release lamps. The metal window frames are unpainted, and form a significant part of the livery.

Below:

No 47711 *County of Hertfordshire* looks resplendent at Crewe on 15 May 1999 while working the 09.15 from Brighton to Manchester and Edinburgh. The style of painting is very similar to that of the Mk 3 carriages illustrated in the previous photographs. Note that the BR-style nameplates are painted with a lighter red background, and that the locomotive number is low-down on the right-end cabside.

all driving vehicles the cab front dome is black as well.

The Virgin logo is placed on the grey area at each end of each carriage and locomotive near the terminations of the three white lines. A much larger version is placed centrally on the red area on the bodysides of HST power cars and DVTs. Vehicle numbers are in white rail alphabet, generally at the right-hand ends of the lower bodysides. First class is denoted by a yellow stripe below the cantrail along the dark grey bodyside area only and wrapping round onto the vehicle ends. The overall effect is most striking.

The first sets of Mk 2 vehicles to be refurbished were outshopped in InterCity livery; because their replacement by Voyager diesel units is imminent, these coaches are expected never to receive Virgin colours.

Virgin Nameplates

Nameplates have been applied to locomotives, HST power cars and locomotive-hauled driving van trailers. The Virgin style uses cast nameplates as per BR, but the lettering is italicised and backgrounds are normally painted red. Special lettering is often used if appropriate to the subject.

Anglia Railways

For those observers whose eyes have difficulty distinguishing shades of blue and green, the Anglia livery of turquoise and white poses a problem: is it blue or is it green? To me it is blue, and I ask readers to whom it appears to be green to accept that eyesight perceptions differ. The base colour is applied on locomotives and locomotive-hauled stock over the bodysides, offset by two white bands, one at cantrail level and one, slightly broader, below the windows. On the locomotives and driving trailer vehicles the '**Anglia**' logo is applied in large, bold, italicised, semi-serif lettering, located in a break in the lower white lining band. On carriage sides it is located under the left-most passenger window. Carriage numbers are in white at the lowest right-hand point of the bodysides. Below the cab windscreens there is a wide yellow warning panel, in which the locomotive number is placed centrally, and that of the driving trailer at the bottom, both in black in what appears to be Gill Sans. On the locomotive the number is at the left end near the bottom, just in front of the cab door. Otherwise, carriage ends are black, roofs dark grey, and everything on or below the underframe is black. Note that the Anglia logo is in white but that the '*i*' is dotted in orange.

This style was adapted for use on the Norwich Crown Point Class 08 diesel shunting locomotive, on which the company logo is affixed to the engine compartment doors and the number is in front of the white band, which is applied only to the cab, below window level. The standard wasp stripes in warning yellow and black are the first the author has seen that comply fully with Railway Group Standard GM/RT2180, which requires *all* forward-facing surfaces above the buffer beam to be striped; Anglia's interpretation puts stripes on the front of the compressor housing, battery box, fuel tank and cab front, as well as conventionally on the radiator housing and cab back.

Above:
Nameplates specifically designed for use on Virgin locomotives, power cars and driving van trailers have italicised lettering. *Brian Morrison*

Above right:
A homogeneous approach to train painting was achieved by Anglia Railways with its locomotive-hauled push-pull Mk 2 sets. All-over turquoise, with a wide lining band below the windows and a narrower one above, the effect is individualistic. Note the curved sides of the warning-yellow panel on the locomotive front. A standard BR-style nameplate with a black background graces the side of the locomotive. Bo-Bo electric No 86235 *Crown Point* **leads the 15.14 from Norwich into Ipswich** *en route* **to London Liverpool Street on 29 June 1999.**

Below right:
A study of the rear of the same train, showing the livery treatment of the Anglia Mk 2 driving trailer vehicles. Note that the 'Anglia**' symbol is larger on the driving car, as well as being placed higher on the bodyside.**

It was not until the year 2000 that the first re-livery of a Class 150 DMU into Anglia style took place. This is similar to the livery applied to Anglia's Mk 2 locomotive-hauled stock, with the following exceptions. Each entrance door is painted white across the window surround; this colour is repeated in vertical bands either side of each doorway, and blends with radii into the upper white lining band. Just below the bodyside windows there is an additional white line, very narrow, which also blends into the vertical white bands. Effectively, the turquoise colour at bodyside window level forms a broad band surrounding the side windows. The bodyside blue is carried on to the upper cab front; the roofs are grey. The gangway seal plate is warning yellow for its full height, but the yellow colour is otherwise only on the lower half of the cab front. The '**Anglia**' logo on these vehicles is on the lower bodysides, midway between the passenger entrance doorways. The overall effect of this livery is fussy.

ScotRail Sleepers

There is some similarity between the ScotRail livery on the company's sleeping cars and that used on its DMUs (see Chapter 2), but not much. The Mk 3 sleeping cars are decked overall in two shades of purple, the darker shade being a very broad band across the bodyside windows, with the lighter purple band lower on the bodyside. Along the top of the body, just above cantrail level (which is marked by an orange OHLE warning line) is a narrow white band, with a similar band drawn along the base of the body. Passenger entrance doors are off-white. A full-body-size version of the ScotRail curved motif in off-white stretches up from the white baseline across two compartment windows and terminates at a blunt angle in the upper white band. There is a very narrow white line between the two purple bands. The 'SCOTRAIL' name appears at the left end of the lower bodyside. Carriage roofs are dark grey. This is an impressively smart livery that breaks with tradition in a number of ways, not least in its choice of colours and in its treatment of the ScotRail logo.

Above:

The Anglia Railways turquoise livery looks well on the diesel shunting locomotive at Norwich Crown Point depot. Note that all forward-facing surfaces have yellow/black wasp stripes. Livery additions include the yellow coupling rods and the white-rimmed wheels and buffers. The light grey cab roof is also unusual. The dot over the 'i' in 'Anglia' is correctly orange.

When Anglia Railways took delivery of its newly-ordered Class 170 DMUs, a significantly changed version of the Anglia livery appeared, and this is described in Chapter 7.

Below:

When ScotRail Railways agreed to take over the Anglo-Scottish sleeping car trains, it upgraded the passenger amenities offered on these long-distance services. A livery suggesting quality has been applied to the vehicles. Dark purple upper panels and lighter purple lower panels on the bodysides are separated by a thin white line, and there are broader white bands above the cantrail and at the base of the bodysides. Vehicle roofs and ends are dark grey. Near the left end of the bodyside is a full-body-height ScotRail emblem in white. To the left of this is the term 'SCOTRAIL' and a small emblem, set in the lighter purple area below the end compartment windows. At the other end of the car is the branding 'CALEDONIAN SLEEPER' in white. Passenger entrance doors are white. *Colin J. Marsden*

2. REGIONAL TRAIN SERVICES

This chapter covers regional train services that operate generally away from the London area (with minor exceptions), starting in North East England, and working through the train operators southwards to the Isle of Wight and finishing with ScotRail which was a late but significant starter in the corporate livery sequence. These were the service groups covered by the former Regional Railways sector of British Rail. Many of these train operators provide services for local Passenger Transport Executives, whose liveries were covered in the previous book *Railway Liveries: BR Traction 1948-1995*. Only the Strathclyde livery changed at about the time of privatisation; this is included in the present book, as is the adaptation of Northern Spirit's corporate livery for West Yorkshire PTE.

Northern Spirit

The 'Big N' could be the tag given colloquially to Northern Spirit's livery, introduced in 1998 in two basic forms. Class 158s allocated to the trans-Pennine routes received branding at the left end of the lower bodysides in non-serif, rounded, lower-case lettering as 'trans**pennine**xpress', the '**e**' at the end of '**pennine**' being common with the first letter of 'express'. The overall bodyside colour is an attractive plum hue that varies significantly to the eye

Below:
Trans-Pennine Express DMU No 158 800 rolls into Manchester Oxford Road on 19 July 2000, working the 11.22 from Liverpool Lime Street to Scarborough. The unit wears the plum livery with the large 'N' symbol that causes Northern Spirit units to stand out visually from the rest.
Tony Miles

according to the angle and quality of light falling on it. Near the right-hand end of each body side is a full-height, very bold capital '***N***' in metallic gold — a most striking image that could quickly raise the profile of Northern Spirit in the public consciousness (were it not for the current likelihood of holding company Arriva's demanding replacement of the new Northern Spirit livery by its own). The company name is expressed modestly as '**NorthernSpirit**', unspaced, in small, white, rounded, non-serif lettering low at the right-hand end of the bodyside. Sensibly, the First-class section is picked out by a gold line above its windows — a sensitive reflection of the former use of a yellow line for this purpose. Vehicle roofs are mid-grey, and the cab front has the top half in black and the lower half, including the obstacle-deflector shield, in warning yellow.

A MetroTrain version of Northern Spirit livery has been applied to West Yorkshire PTE-owned Class 158s. In this case, the plum colour is replaced by MetroTrain red and the big '***N***' is metallic silver. The MetroTrain motif is at the left lower end of the bodyside before the entrance doors. This style has been adapted for the new Class 333 electric multiple-units for the Leeds-Bradford-Ilkley triangle, the major change being the application of yellow to the sliding entrance doors in response to a requirement in the Disability Discrimination Regulations that

Above:
The branding of the Trans-Pennine Express trains runs the words together in both white and gold lettering. A gold stripe near cantrail level indicates the position of First class in the train.

Right:
New Class 333 EMUs were delivered in the same red livery as DMU No 158 909, but with two differences. One is that the vehicles' design has black ribbon-glazing along the bodysides. Secondly, the passenger access doors have been coloured yellow to make them easier to find. The vehicle roof and upper cab front are black, and the warning yellow is carried down over the obstacle-deflector spoiler. The overall effect is not homogeneous! No 333 002 was on display at Leeds on 26 April 2000. *Brian Morrison*

entrance doors be easily identifiable to people with poor eyesight; this has the unfortunate effect of wrecking the symmetry of the new MetroTrain livery.

A third version of the Northern Spirit livery stands out from the other two. The stopping-train services that are worked by Class 142 to 144 'Pacer' and 156 'Super Sprinter' units are being painted light blue overall, with the large Northern Spirit '***N***' in lime green. At the left lower end of the bodyside the company name appears in medium-sized, rounded lettering, unspaced, 'Northern' being in lime green

and 'Spirit' in white. Initial capitals are used in this case. On these classes the obstacle-deflector shield is painted black. Those units allocated to Nexus (Tyne

& Wear PTE) services have additionally the Nexus symbol at the right end of the left-hand car, level with the 'NorthernSpirit' motif. Vehicle numbers are in white rail alphabet, placed at the bottom edge of the bodysides, at the outer ends of the 'Pacer' units and the inner ends of the 'Sprinters'.

These three liveries use form rather than colour to pick out the Northern Spirit style, the main impact being the use of the large-logo '***N***' as a visual break in the otherwise-plain overall bodyside colour. Thus the blue Class 156s are just as easily identified as Northern Spirit units as are the red Class 158s.

North Western Trains

North Western Trains' first new train livery appeared on the Class 322 electric multiple-units leased for the abortive London Euston services from Manchester Airport. This used what the company describes as 'Navy blue' overall on the bodysides and inner ends. Relief and some impact came from the application of large stars in pearlescent gold across the driving cabs, and even bigger ones splashed across the bodyside ends of adjoining carriages. The star at the cab end had an arm that reached up to cantrail level, from which a gold band led back along the full length of the train, terminating in the star at the other end of the unit. (An unusual feature is that the orange OHLE warning line runs through the middle of this gold band.) The motif '***north western trains***' in white italic, sans-serif lettering was placed on the lower bodyside midway between the passenger

entrance doorways, with a gold crescent sweeping round the left end of the motif and a star above the word '**north**'. Four smaller stars placed in line decorated each passenger entrance doorway. Vehicle numbers were in white rail alphabet at the right-hand end of each car, except on the right-end car, where the number was at the left — an arrangement that is becoming standard across most companies. All vehicle numbers were placed just below the windows. The cab front, unlike the treatment of Classes 321 and 322 elsewhere, was all-over warning yellow (including the obstacle-deflector) but with a narrow black surround to the front windscreens. The carriage roofs were painted blue.

The Class 322 units were eventually returned off-lease and transferred back to West Anglia Great Northern. However, their North Western Trains livery style spread to a few Class 323 EMUs and to a number of 'Sprinter' and 'Pacer' DMU sets. On at least one of the '323s' an attempt was made to take the gold line over the roof, but as this was out of reach of carriage washing machines, the initially-smart effect was not sustained.

The advent of the holding company, FirstGroup, with its policy of imprinting its image on its subsidiaries' products, brought a change to the liveries of new North Western trains, as will be described in Chapter 7. The Greater Manchester PTE-funded trains have not been re-liveried since privatisation, the only change being the addition of the First North Western logo.

Merseyrail Electrics
Merseyrail Electrics inherited a striking yellow livery from its time in the Regional Railways sector of British Rail, and sensibly retained this relatively new

style after privatisation, merely removing the Regional Railways insignia with its minute BR double-arrow. This livery is described in *Railway Liveries: BR Traction 1948-1995*. A change initiated during repaints early in 2001 is the omission of the bodyside black lining band.

Central Trains

Central Trains waited almost until its new Class 170 'Turbostar' DMUs appeared before launching its new company style on a surprised public. Passengers, for many years used to various shades of grey and blue, are now confronted with the brightest green to appear on a train since LNER apple green was abandoned after BR was born! The colour is close to apple green but more 'yellow'. The bright green is offset by a dark green band along the bottom of the bodyside. A novel feature is the bright blue area on the cab front and upper sides that sweeps up from just in front of the lamp clusters to surround the warning-yellow cab front, and on the cabsides crosses the side window and then blends with the cantrail-level roof line. The blue and bright green areas are separated by a red line that levels out at the cantrail gutter, continuing along the vehicle length. The orange OHLE warning line is immediately below and adjoining the red gutter.

To meet the needs of the poorly-sighted, the passenger entrance doors are painted warning yellow

Above:
Before complete new liveries were adopted by the Central Trains franchise, the company's name appeared on some of its multiple-units in this form, using light blue capital lettering partially embraced at one end by a green symbol of four tapered semi-circles. This is on a Class 156 DMU.

Above right:
A Class 158 DMU approaches Derby on the 07.09 from Chester to Lincoln Central on 31 May 1999, showing off its new Central Trains colours of two-tone green. A blue area sweeps up across the cabside windows to merge with the roof line above the first pair of entrance doors. The roof is black. The unit is striking in appearance despite the clutter of insignia and messages on the lower bodysides.

Right:
The treatment of Central Trains' new Class 170 DMUs was smarter, with a stronger sweep of blue on the cabsides that also embraced the cab front. This view shows clearly the red lining that separates the blue from the bright green colour and which, according to its stylist, 'acts as a catalyst and fires all the colours together'. These two units were at Derby on 13 September 1999. Note that the bottoms of the passenger entrance doors are bright green, whereas on the Class 158 they are dark green. The 'CENTRAL' lettering is now in dark blue, and the logo is in white with only three semi-circles.

from a line level with the top of the windows downwards to line up with the top of the dark green band. Above and below the yellow area, the doors are bright green. Although the blue paint on the cab

includes the front roof dome, the rest of the vehicle roofs are dark grey.

The Central Trains logo, with the name in plain, blue sans-serif capitals and with a motif of white, concentric crescents, appears at each end of each car below the ribbon-glazed windows. In addition there is a motto 'go', also with crescents, and a telephone number (0870 000 60 60) emblazoned across the body between the doorways and below the windows, giving a somewhat cluttered appearance; only the brightness of the overall livery prevents this offending the eye. Vehicle numbers appear in white rail alphabet at the bottom of the bodysides at the inner ends of each unit, and the unit number appears in the usual place under the driver's windscreen, but in this case with thinner-than-standard numerals.

A similar style has been adopted for repainted Class 156 and 158 units, except that the blue area is reduced and the cab front is painted similarly to the Northern Spirit Class 158s (apart from a green band across the bottom of the obstacle-deflector on the Central Trains units). Because the '156s' and '158s' do not have dark ribbon glazing, a very dark grey band has been painted across the window area.

Central Trains did not re-livery the Centro (West Midlands PTE)-sponsored Class 323 EMUs and '150' DMUs; their livery style was described in *Railway Liveries: BR Traction 1948-1995*.

Above:
Only Central Trains was brave enough to apply its telephone hot-line number to the carriage sides! The livery uses bright and dark greens, with yellow to mark out the entrance doors, offset by dark ribbon glazing.

Above right:
Wales & West did not re-livery any of its stock until the year 2000. Minimal re-branding took place through the application of decals carrying the 'Wales & West' name in black serif lettering, alongside which was a pale blue and white symbol of converging and diverging rails. This Class 143 'Pacer' was seen at Cardiff on 4 March 1999.

Right:
The Wales & West Class 158-operated services between Cardiff and Nottingham and to Portsmouth and Brighton were marketed under the brand name 'Alphaline'. A strong motif for this was applied to the units (albeit on the former BR Regional Railways livery), placed behind the cab-end doorway on each vehicle.

Wales & West

Wales & West was very late in applying a new livery to its trains, having been content to continue for almost five years with the Regional Railways colours, albeit with modest re-branding.

The new livery emerged as the Class 158 units that operate the 'Alphaline' services from Cardiff to Nottingham and Manchester began a programme of

repainting in 2000. The chosen style was an overall mid-grey on the bodysides with wrap-round yellow areas across the entrance doors at each vehicle end.

It is best described by reference to the illustrations, as those show clearly the style of logo adopted. Whether such a large grey area will remain attractive in the longer term remains to be seen; one recalls the zest with which Thameslink removed the grey livery from its Class 319 units after privatisation.

Cardiff Railways

Thankfully just in time to be included in this book, Cardiff Railways unveiled its new livery for 'Pacer' DMUs late in 2000. The colours are drawn from the Welsh national flag, being red, mid-green and white. There is a red band along the base of the bodysides, excluding the entrance doors. The rest of the bodyside area is basically a green panel with white lining bands above and below. Additionally there is a broad white band below the bodyside windows, terminating below the cab side windows in a 180û curve. On the outer and upper edges of this white band there is a narrow pale green line — the same green with which the passenger entrance doors are painted.

Cardiff Railways is marketed as 'Valley Lines'. This term appears in red midway along each bodyside, the two words separated by a dragon logo in outline red; below the dragon, the green and white bodyside lining is dipped at an angle of 45°. The dragon also appears as a metallic silver decal that overlaps the passenger windows adjacent to each driving cab, as well as in white outline centrally below the cab front windscreen. Vehicle roofs are grey, and everything from solebars downwards is black. The cab front is warning yellow, finished off vertically at the bodyside join, but with black surrounds to the windscreens.

This is an attractive livery, quite different from anything else, and patriotically capable of forming the prototype livery for an all-Wales railway franchise, should one be required at re-franchising. I wonder if it will.

Island Line

Until 1999 the former London Underground 1938 stock that works on the Isle of Wight remained in its Network SouthEast colours. For the 2000 summer service the majority received aggressively-designed blue and yellow vinyl sheets printed with a dinosaur theme. This was aimed at attracting younger people to the trains, and appears to have been successful. The livery is best studied from the illustrations. It remains a unique approach to railway marketing.

ScotRail Railways

The first livery change in Scotland came at about the time of privatisation, but was not connected with it. Strathclyde Passenger Transport Executive became disenchanted with its 'Strathclyde red' (orange) and black livery, and decided to adopt a more traditional style. The result was a copy of British Railways' 1949 carmine and cream livery, lined out in black edged with cream, the red being below and above the windows and the cream being the broad band across the window areas. The red is certainly much darker than the original carmine (more like crimson, which

was how BR described its carmine!), and readers must judge for themselves whether the style fits the more modern body shapes of Class 303, 314 and 318 EMUs and Class 156 DMUs. New symbols for Strathclyde Transport and ScotRail have been applied, as seen in the accompanying photograph. Strathclyde is the only PTE to have adopted a brand-new and independent livery style in the period covered by this book.

ScotRail itself waited until its new Class 170 DMUs were due to be delivered before embarking on its new style, which is one of the most individualistic styles to be adopted by any train operator. The base colours are off-white with a purple band across the window areas — a colour that is repeated on the entrance doors, which are purple overall. The

Above:

ScotRail Railways burst forth in 1999 with a new livery that remains individualistic. This view of Class 170 and 158 units coupled together at Edinburgh on a Glasgow service on 1 December 2000 shows key common features as well as minor differences in layout and proportion. ScotRail breaks with tradition from the purple roofs downwards. Just below the cantrail is a wide white band (actually bleeding above the cantrail on the '170', on the right), below which is a red band that leans towards dark orange in hue. Below that on the '158' is a deep purple band across the windows, whereas the '170' has its black ribbon-glazing, except that the cabside window band is purple. Then

follows a green band, again separated by a narrow white lining band, and the lower bodyside is white. On the Class 170 the cab-front spoiler is white, whereas on the '158' it is warning yellow. That is because the '158' cab front is all-over yellow but the 'Turbostar' follows Adtranz's standard layout for the warning panel. Entrance doors are purple. There is on each alternate bodyside a full-height representation of the ScotRail flash with a broad white area containing, below the window line, the term 'SCOTRAIL' in purple followed by a small version of the flash. On the '158' the 'SCOTRAIL' lettering is larger than on the '170'. On the other coaches the company name is placed in a white gap in the green band.

Right:

Treatment of the Class 156 units in Scotland is similar to that of the '158s'. This view of No 156 474 at Edinburgh on 31 October 2000 also shows (right) part of the cab front on a 'Turbostar'. On the '156' the obstacle-deflector shield is painted warning yellow, and the purple of the vehicle roof is brought down to include the edge of the cab front. On this class the metal window frames are left unpainted.

45

window band has above and adjacent a narrower red lining band, while above this is a white band bordering the gutter. The gutter forms part of the OHLE warning line continuum, but in this case ScotRail has obtained a concession from Railtrack whereby the warning line is painted ScotRail red, not orange. This is in deference to matching a livery in which colour contrasts are key. Below the windows, only slightly separated from the purple band, is a pale emerald green band. Near one end of each two-car unit, or both ends of a three-car set, is a full-body-height representation of the current ScotRail logo, beyond which is a totally white area. The placement of the full-height logo and white area differs considerably on different classes, due to the location of entrance doors. A smaller logo and the

Above:
A Class 150/2 DMU at Edinburgh on 31 October 2000 shows a simpler version of the ScotRail livery for suburban use. The red and green bands are narrower and placed differently, and the 'SCOTRAIL' logo appears forward on the white lower bodyside.

term 'SCOTRAIL' appear in a gap in the green band, midway along one vehicle in each unit. Carriage roofs are purple, and the yellow cab fronts carry black around the windscreens. There is a change for the Class 150 units used on stopping and Edinburgh suburban services. These have a wide off-white area below the windows on which the legend 'ScotRail' is placed at the left end. All versions of the livery are certainly eye-catching. Photographs do not do the style justice. One has to see the real thing to appreciate its overall effect.

ScotRail Nameplates

ScotRail always tried to keep sweet its relations with major customers and opinion-formers by naming locomotives. Now that it is largely a multiple-unit railway, ScotRail has extended the practice to EMUs and DMUs, using cast plates on the sides of the units just below the passenger windows nearest the driving ends. The plates are cast aluminium with black backing, and have capital sans-serif lettering.

High Road
20th Anniversary 2000

Above:
ScotRail Railways has named several multiple-unit sets. This nameplate is affixed to EMU No 320 308. *Brian Morrison*

3. LONDON-CENTRED REGIONAL AND SUBURBAN SERVICES

The Train Operating Companies whose liveries are described in this chapter are those that were formed out of BR's Network SouthEast business. They are dealt with in this book in an anti-clockwise order around London, starting at the Thames estuary with the London, Tilbury & Southend TOC and completing the circuit with Connex.

LTS Rail

This small, Southend-based franchise has in its short life had three liveries for multiple-units! The first was a simple adaptation of the Network SouthEast style that enabled it to stamp its mark on existing Class 312 and 317 EMUs. The blue band across the windows was retained, as was the mid-grey at the bottom of the bodysides and the upper

and lower white bands. Even the narrow red line that had replaced the orange OHLE warning line on

Below:
To achieve a quick visual change on its Class 317 EMUs, LTS Rail commissioned stylist Best Impressions to design a simple adaptation of the BR Network SouthEast livery. Using vinyl decals, a green line replaced the lower NSE red band. The warning-yellow panel shape was adjusted behind the cabsides in the fashion of the earlier Class 313, 314 and 315 sets, and the white and green lines brought to a point near the lower cab front. The effect was a different livery which could be applied easily at a maintenance depot, but which was devoid of any exterior service or ownership branding. No 317 302 arrives at Barking on the 13.50 from London Fenchurch Street to Southend Central via Tilbury on 19 April 1999.

NSE-liveried trains was retained. The lower red band was replaced by a mid-green band and there was modified treatment of the cabside area. This made use of the warning-yellow cut-away at the body end corners, the blue, white and green parts of the style being made to flow away from it. The photographs illustrate this better than words can describe.

The LTS line's second livery was that adopted on its first new 'Electrostar' Class 357 EMUs. Barely had the first units entered traffic in summer 2000 when the franchise was re-launched with a new brand name and a completely new corporate style. These liveries are described in Chapter 7.

First Great Eastern

Great Eastern's off-white, grey, blue and green livery comes in two key varieties, one each for its Class 321 and 315 EMUs. That on the '321s' keeps parts of the NSE livery, namely the light grey body and the blue

window band. There is at the unit ends a sweep of
colour: dark blue and green colours have been
applied in widening stripes that rise up and over the
window blue band. The top colour, when the sweep
ends and becomes a set of parallel lines, is dark blue,
below which (though still above the bodyside
windows) is a broader green band. Below the
windows is a dark blue band bordering the NSE
blue, then a light grey area, and finally a green band
above the lowest grey area at the bottom of the
bodyside. The GE dark blue is slightly darker than
the NSE dark blue, though this may be due to
difficulty in matching the decals to the paint. The
orange warning line has been lifted slightly by
means of a zig-zag just behind and above the cab
door.

The legend '**Great Eastern**' is placed in blue
FirstGroup corporate bold sans-serif lettering,
followed by a blue version of the group's '*f*' symbol, at
all non-driving ends of the vehicle bodysides below
the passenger end windows; this also appears above
the cab end passenger window at the Standard-class
end of the unit. There is a variation at the First-class
end. Here the word '**First**' is placed, again in bold
blue lettering, followed by the '*f*' symbol in red, then
by the words 'Great Eastern', the latter written
smaller and in regular (rather than bold) typeface. At
the First-class end there is also a gold-coloured five-
sided shape in front of the cab door which

Above:
**The First Great Eastern livery applied to the inner-
suburban Class 315 units was different from but
identifiable with that on the '321s'. No 315 809, at
Shenfield on 15 April 1997 (the day the livery was
launched), shows the effective use of grey, dark blue
and green stripes sweeping up behind the white
cabside, with the mid-grey colour being extended to
the lower-bodyside area along the train. The window
band is the same blue colour as the stripe.** *Colin J. Marsden*

presumably is the main indicator of the First-class
section. There is also a small '**First**' and red '*f*' on the
cab fronts, just above the centre coupling. Carriage
roofs are light grey.

The style for the inner-suburban Class 315 units is
visually different. On these units the cabsides and
surrounds are basically white. Light grey, blue and
green bands flow from the lower cab front up the
sides of the leading vehicles, but in this case the top
band at the edge of the roof line is light grey. The
blue disappears so that there is a green band just
above the passenger windows. The window band
itself is dark blue, and there is a green line below
that. The lower bodyside is light grey. Treatment of
the cab front is interesting: the light grey flowing
band starts as a surround to the tail- and marker-
lamp clusters, while below this and stretching across

Above:
For its Class 317s West Anglia Great Northern uses a buttermilk-based livery, offset by sweeps of dark blue and yellow, with passenger doorways in bright red. The warning yellow of the cab front has been curved back around the bodyside edge, and the windscreen surround is black. No 317 666 arrives at Finsbury Park with the 16.50 London King's Cross-Peterborough semi-fast on 10 April 2000.

the bottom of the cab front are blue and green lines; the cab windscreen surround is black, and the rest of the cab front is warning yellow except where the white colour is brought over the top to border the orange warning line above the cab windows. 'Great Eastern' and the '*f*' symbol are on the bodysides as before, except that those at the vehicle bodyside ends are of the bold '**First**', red '*f*' and smaller 'Great Eastern' style used at the First-class ends of the Class 321s.

Neither livery style makes any attempt at picking out visually the passenger access doors, so some future change to this livery may be expected.

West Anglia Great Northern

The West Anglia Great Northern (WAGN) Train Operating Company adopted a relatively simple livery that has had surprisingly good impact. The overall colour on the bodysides is a pale shade of ivory (classified as 'buttermilk'), offset by a deep blue band along the bodyside bottom edges. The blue and ivory are separated by a wide lining band in yellow — a colour that is repeated in a narrower lining band above the First-class section but well spaced below the standard orange warning line. Roofs are dark grey. A panel of executive dark grey is used to extend the visual line of the bodyside windows. To make the passenger access doors highly visible, these have been painted red from the roof gutter down to just above the lower yellow lining band. Note that the red colour covers not just the doors but also about 4in of bodyside either side of the doors. At the bodyside ends there is a swathe of executive dark grey that starts across the bottom of the cab front and curves upwards over and behind the cab door to the bodyside roof, widening as it does so, to form a speed curve that separates the warning-yellow cab front from the rest of the vehicle livery. From a point at the bottom end corner, the lower bodyside livery lines all diverge and quickly take up their parallel positions along the unit. The cab-front treatment is deliberately plain: a black area surrounding the windscreen and crossing the gangway end, thus minimising the blank physical shape of the front end. The warning-yellow area extends a little on to the bodysides in a sweep that

51

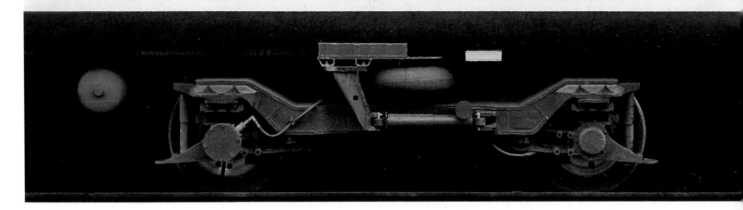

Above left:
**A detail of No 317 670 at London Liverpool Street station,
showing the passenger door livery treatment. Note that the
red extends outside the sliding doors to the sides and top of
the bodyside around the doorways. There is a yellow band
over the First-class section, placed below the orange OHLE
warning line. The WAGN Railway company symbol and
initials appear each side of each doorway.**

Left:
**Buttermilk was the base colour used on the WAGN
Class 322 units used for the Stansted Skytrain Express
Rail Link service. Other decoration is limited to the gold
band along the lower bodyside. The brand name is placed
in black italic serif lettering in a gap in this band.
No 322 482 had been transferred away from WAGN by the
time this photograph was taken at London Euston on
3 February 1999.**

Above:
**Thameslink applied its website address to all units during
the summer of 2000.**

owes its origin to the bodyside cut-away that exists
for gauging reasons on Class 313, 314 and 315 units.
The WAGN company logo is placed small on the
dark grey panels alongside the entrance doors. The
overall effect is remarkably successful, as it turns
what is truly a plain, unimaginatively-shaped
electric multiple-unit into a train with an aura of
quality.

For the dedicated Class 322 electric multiple-units
used on its service to Stansted Airport, WAGN opted
for a plain, overall light grey livery
(indistinguishable from the later buttermilk), offset
by a dark blue lining band at cantrail level, aligned
with the orange warning line, and a gold lining band,
low on the bodyside, starting from the front of the
cab door and running back along the unit. The brand
name 'Stansted Sky*train*' is placed in a gap in the
gold band at the right-hand end of the bodyside,
applied in dark blue serif lettering; a blue and gold
motif separates the two words. Immediately below
the word 'Sky*train*' is placed, in small, widely-spaced
sans-serif letters, the legend 'EXPRESS RAIL LINK', the
position of which causes the tail of the 'y' of
'Sky*train*' to be cut short. There is no colour contrast
to pick out the passenger entrance doors, the roofs
are dark grey, and the cab front has just the plastic
panel below the windscreen in warning yellow, all
else being black above and light grey below the
windscreen, except for some black around the lamp
clusters as per former NSE practice.

Thameslink

Almost defiantly, Thameslink stamped its image on
its dual-voltage Class 319 EMUs by quickly
eliminating the unpopular grey livery that BR had
applied in its last days. Indeed, the grey disappeared
almost two years before the remaining NSE-liveried

units were repainted! The principal colour adopted is a deep shade of dark blue, which covers the bodysides, cab fronts and roofs. This is offset by a deep yellow band along the bodysides midway between the bottom of the passenger windows and the bodyside baseline, the yellow band being flanked by white lining. At the front end the yellow warning colour surrounds the windscreens, but stops short of the lamp clusters. Below the warning yellow is a

band of dark blue, which is carried round to the bodysides and swept up at an acute angle, widening sharply to form the blue band across the windows. The white/yellow/white band along the bodysides narrows sharply in front of the cab doors to form a narrow white band across the base of the cab front. There is also white lining across the top of the blue window band, extending up to the orange warning line.

The brand name '***THAMESLINK***' is placed in dark blue on the golden yellow band centrally on the bodysides of all coaches. It also appears in yellow, high alongside both sides of the passenger access doorways, subscripted by the service brand (eg '*CITYFLIER*'). First class is denoted by yellow italic lettering under the end passenger window of the First-class section, and a large figure '1' by the appropriate entrance doorway. On the cab front of CityFlyer units there is a triangular logo placed on the blue band on the central escape door, and this is repeated very small above the Thameslink branding at the doorways. CityMetro inner-suburban units have an elliptical logo in yellow edged in white with a blue 'M'. The unit number is in black serif numerals at the bottom of the warning-yellow area below the driver's window.

Despite the darkness of the blue, and perhaps because of the contrast between it and the golden yellow, this livery is smart and has considerable appeal. It has even successfully overcome the blandness of the Class 319 front-end design by dint of

breaking up the shape of the cab front with the different areas of yellow, blue and white.

Silverlink

Silverlink hired design firm Best Impressions and was rewarded with a livery that stands out from the rest. Dark purple — a colour described in the ICI catalogue as 'Cadbury's purple' — forms the basis. The bottom edge of the bodysides has a bright green band, separated from the purple by white lining. At the cab ends, white lining and green band sweep up from the bottom edge to form a wide wave across and behind the cab door, levelling out at the first passenger access doorway. The top of the wave on the Class 313s is surmounted by a symbolic flying bird in white and silver-grey. Recognition of the need for doorways to be visible to the partially-sighted gives rise to the passenger access doors' being painted warning yellow above the white lining, the yellow being carried up on the bodysides above the doorways to the roof gutter (or an equivalent height on the Class 321). On the Class 313 cab front, the warning-yellow area is much the same as it was under NSE, except that below the head, marker and tail lamps is a purple band, and the central escape door area is purple all the way down from roof level. The warning horns are finished in grey — a neat touch. The Class 321 cab front follows typical NSE lines with the warning yellow restricted to the panel

Above:
On the Class 313 inner-suburban units working the North London lines there is no green stripe on the cab front (only purple), and the warning-yellow area is almost full-frontal apart from the vertical purple band over the central escape door. The unit number is in black rail alphabet. The bird symbol in this application flies above the green and white sweep behind the cabside, and the branding is 'silverlink metro'. **The window frames are left in polished metal. No 313 121 was working a North Woolwich to Richmond train at Gospel Oák on 19 April 1999.**

below the windscreen, except that below the yellow panel the bodyside bright green band is carried across the bottom of the cab front. Carriage roofs are dark grey.

On the green part of the wave is the branding 'silverlink metro' or 'silverlink county' in purple sans-serif rail alphabet-style regular and narrow lettering. On the Class 321s the branding is preceded by the flying bird symbol. The First-class sections on the Class 321 units are announced by large white '1' figures on the bodysides, high up on either side of the appropriate doorways.

The same livery style has been successfully adapted to the Class 150 DMUs assigned to the Watford, Bedford and Gospel Oak services, but for these it is the purple colour that is continued across under the yellow warning area on the cab front, and

56

Above:
For the Class 150 'Sprinter' DMUs transferred in for the Gospel Oak-Barking service and for the Bedford-Bletchley line, the livery treatment was similar to that of the Class 313 electric units, except that the bodyside branding is simply '**silverlink**'. No 150 129 was at Barking on 13 October 2000.

Right:
Some early privatised operators applied colours that harked back to those used by BR. There was for instance a clear affinity between Chiltern Railways' livery on its brand-new Class 168 DMUs (the first new passenger trains delivered to a private operator) and that of the former Network SouthEast. The blue window band is there, though angled over the cabside, and there is a small red lining band near the bottom of the bodyside. Some doorways have yellow tops. No 168 005 waits to leave London Marylebone on 10 April 2000 with the 15.53 service to Birmingham Snow Hill.

on these units the obstacle-deflector is painted yellow. A special version of the Silverlink livery was formerly applied to a Class 121 'bubble car' DMU (see Appendix B), and another has been applied to a diesel shunting locomotive used at Bletchley depot.

Chiltern Railways

While to date the Chiltern Railways company has not re-liveried its inherited Class 165 DMUs, it did apply a new style to the Class 168 and 170 units it received new from Adtranz. The new colours recognise Chiltern's Network SouthEast origins, and indeed do not look out of place when a new unit is coupled in multiple with a '165'. The bodysides, ends and roofs are white overall, with a dark blue band across the windows. Apart from the obligatory overhead line electrification (OHLE) orange warning line, the only other lining is a narrow red line across the white area low on the bodysides. This terminates with the 'Chiltern Railways' branding in blue serif upper- and lower-case lettering which is underlined in red with a small flourish of double underlining at the right-hand end of the branding. The cab ends follow the modern standard, with the windscreen surrounds in black and the warning yellow restricted to the panel below the windscreen. Of note is the forward rake of the end of the blue area in front of the cab doors. The top strip of the passenger entrance doors at the First-class end of the unit is a yellow decal strip, though not all units originally had this in place.

Thames Trains

Of all the Train Operating Companies formed directly from the privatisation of British Rail, Thames Trains was the last but one to launch a new livery. The first repainted Class 166 DMU to emerge in a new style appeared in the summer of 2000. This is yet another London livery that holds faithfully to the NSE blue window band, this time terminated with a semi-oval curve across and in front of the cab doors. The overall body colour is otherwise white, extending to the carriage roofs. Passenger entrance doors are largely covered by a diagonal splash of lime green that picks them out for everyone, including the partially-sighted. The cab front is liveried with the windscreen surrounds in black, a yellow warning panel with rounded outer ends above the coupler, and a dark blue band separating them and carrying the unit number in its unchanged position.

The service branding for what was previously 'Turbo Express' is now 'Thames Trains Express', and this is applied to each coach on the white area under the windows. First comes the new '*TT*' logo (see

photograph), which is followed by '**THAMES**' in dark blue, '**TRAINS**' in lime green and '**EXPRESS**' in orange. For once, the First-class section is denoted by a yellow lining band above the windows of the appropriate section of the end power car. The brand name is applied in full in larger lettering in the centre of the lower bodyside on the middle coach of each three-car unit.

Heathrow Express

As the first new passenger-train operator not to be a franchisee, Heathrow Express might have been expected to adopt an original approach to train liveries. There is indeed something of the airliner in the style which the company has adopted for its new Class 332 electric multiple-units. The vehicle base colour is metallic silver-grey overall, offset by black side-window ribbon glazing and royal blue farings between the bogies; otherwise the only other colour used is the black on bogies, underframe equipment (mostly out of sight) and couplings. The silver-grey is extended down to the small, angular farings over the bogies, and to the covers over the unit-end overriders and obstacle-deflectors, making the front of the unit appear somewhat clumsy.

Heathrow Express had attempted to be the first train operator to dispense with the warning yellow panel on cab fronts, as the company wanted to emphasise the sleek outline of its units. Railtrack did not permit this, however, and so the yellow panel was applied almost as a design afterthought by use of plastic decals above and below the divider that lies between the front lamp clusters and the windscreen itself. Indeed, a strip of the decal had to be affixed to the lowest part of the windscreen glass in order to provide the required vertical dimension of yellow to meet the Railway Group Standard. (In the event of this decal's lifting, the area of yellow is compromised — see illustration.) Unit numbers are applied to the cab front in black rail-alphabet numerals on the silver-grey area below the headlamp on the driver's side. The OHLE orange warning line is applied in strict accordance with the Railway Group Standard at the same height all round the unit and just overlapping the top of the driver's windscreen.

The brand name 'Heathrow Express' is applied in the middle of the bodysides on the grey below the window band. 'Heathrow' is in dark grey regular sans-serif lettering. The word '**express**' is applied in very large, mid-grey, bold sans-serif, partly-rounded lettering. At each end of each coach is the company symbol: a pair of opposing, curved-tapered arrows — one white, one mauve — formed into a cross in the centre of a large, dark blue spot. First-class areas are denoted by the words 'FIRST CLASS' at the bottom of the window glazing central to each window using small, sans-serif spaced-out white letters; the tail of the 'R' is extended in a short flare.

Other external livery details include 'Emergency exit' applied in very small white lettering on the

appropriate window panes. The westernmost carriage of each four-car unit has been designated a 'quiet coach' where passengers may not annoy others with the ringing of their mobile telephones. To identify these vehicles, Heathrow Express has had a large white, bold letter '**Q**' fixed to the middle of the glazing of each plug door (ie two to each doorway).

South West Trains

South West Trains (SWT) soon repainted most of its Class 455 inner-suburban electric multiple-units, and then proceeded to re-livery its older Mk 1 stock from Classes 411, 421 and 423. The style used the corporate colours of the holding company, Stagecoach, laid out similarly to the former Network SouthEast colours which the units previously carried. The dark Network blue across the window areas is replaced by Stagecoach's slightly lighter blue. Above that is a white band bordering the gutter, which itself is painted as the orange OHLE warning line (formerly omitted on most BR Southern Region DC electric multiple-units). Below the blue area are three wide bands, of red, orange and off-white, separated by narrow white lines. As another throwback to NSE livery, the red, orange and off-white bands are angled up over the cabsides. Cab fronts are painted overall warning yellow as previously, the '455s' having some black bordering around the cab windscreens. Roofs are dark grey, and everything from the solebars down is black.

South West Trains has had two attempts at displaying its corporate title on trains. Initially it used a white panel placed midway along the bodyside below the windows, bridging the white and red bands on NSE-liveried stock. This carried, in large, dark blue, slightly italic lettering, the initials 'SWT'. On this the 'W' had its two middle strokes crossed at the upper ends, the overlap being expressed as an inverted orange triangle (see illustration). Below 'SWT' appeared the legend 'SOUTH WEST TRAINS' in fine lettering with small serifs. This style of logo was sometimes accompanied by placement on the NSE white band below the windows, towards the right end of the carriage, of the term 'A **STAGECOACH** COMPANY' in dark blue, plain sans-serif capital letters, the word '**STAGECOACH**' being in bolder typeface than the rest. Both these symbols of SWT's presence and ownership were changed before the SWT/Stagecoach livery style had been widely applied.

Left:
South West Trains was reasonably swift in spreading the new Stagecoach colours on its inner-suburban Class 455 units. The colours were the lighter blue, red and orange used on buses, rearranged to fit in with the prevailing NSE livery style, so that when the two liveries were seen on units coupled in multiple neither looked out of place. Units 5719 and 5742 pass each other on Windsor line services near Vauxhall station on 18 September 1997.

Below:
South West Trains' first branding of Network SouthEast-painted EMUs was to blank-out the NSE branding and to apply a panel with the initials 'S W T' in slender serif lettering with 'SOUTH WEST TRAINS' underneath. This panel was normally placed midway along the bodyside below the windows, bridging the white and red lining bands. On a few units the additional wording 'A STAGECOACH COMPANY' was applied to indicate corporate ownership. This view is of the branding on a Class 159 DMU, seen at Waterloo in March 1999.

Towards the right end of the red livery band on the new Stagecoach style is now set the name '**SOUTH WEST** TRAINS'; the words '**SOUTH WEST**' are in bold, sans-serif lettering closed up so that the letters within each word touch one another. The word 'TRAINS' is in narrow orange letters, the capital 'I' being dotted with a small red dot placed in the white line above. The vehicle numbers are also placed on the red band, in standard white rail-alphabet numerals.

When SWT had its 'flagship' Class 442 and 159 multiple-units refurbished, with a substantial improvement to their interior appointment, a suitably striking livery was commissioned from

Left:
Along with the new South West Trains livery of blue, white, red and orange came a better way of expressing the company name, albeit this time without any reference to holding company Stagecoach. Note that the bold lettering runs all the letters in each word together, with no spaces between them, and that the crossbar on the capital 'T' is chamfered at the left end. The narrow lettering of 'TRAINS' is in orange, with a red dot above the capital 'I'.

Below:
One of the most striking train liveries was that adopted by South West Trains for its flagship Class 442 EMUs. The flare of bright red is separated from the bodyside white by a broadening orange band, with the colours going right over the roof — an absolutely original arrangement. Unit 2405 was calling at Bournemouth with the 13.41 from Poole to London Waterloo on 11 July 1998.

Above:
This detail view of unit 2402 at Bournemouth on 12 December 1999 shows the SWT company branding, this time in blue and orange on the white background above the bodyside windows. Note the positioning of the orange OHLE warning line above cantrail level.

graphic designer Best Impressions. The result, in the author's opinion, is Britain's finest train livery. Still using the Stagecoach corporate colours, though changed in proportion, shade and impact, the predominant vehicle colour this time (in terms of area covered) is off-white. Along the units the bodysides have a broad blue band at the base with a narrow orange lining band just inside the upper edge of the blue. The window band is painted a much darker blue which stretches between the inner edges of the swing plug doors, with the exception of the drivers' doors (see next paragraph). The vehicle roof is off-white as well, and the orange OHLE warning line is present in full accordance with the Railway Group Standard. The passenger access doors are painted red from the top down to a point just above the position of the bodyside blue area and orange lining, both of which are carried across the door bottom with a white strip between them and the main area of red. The branding '**SOUTH WEST** TRAINS'

is applied above the left end passenger window just below cantrail level, with the words '**SOUTH WEST**' in dark blue and 'TRAINS' in orange with the capital 'I' dotted in red as before.

It is the treatment of the driving-end coaches in each five-car unit that breaks new ground in British train liveries, if not in world liveries. Ray Stenning of Best Impressions wanted these high-quality trains to catch the eye of passers-by. He achieved this by designing a sweep of strong, bright red from the cab front and reaching the roof, sweeping up from just above the buffers across the first and second passenger bodyside windows and up on to the roof which it crosses in a sweeping curve. An orange band, starting from a point at the bottom corner of the bodyside end, also sweeps up below the red band, widening as it goes further back, crossing the second and third passenger windows, and again curving across the carriage roof above the fifth and sixth windows. At the bottom end of the bodyside, all the lower-bodyside and lining colours start from the same point and sweep up to their respective continuous positions along the bodysides. The cab front is also red, down to just below the cab windscreens. The warning-yellow area crosses the cab front below the windscreens, although the trades unions did not like the gangway-end having red on its upper half. The resultant vertical yellow slab

Above:
This scene at New Milton on 12 June 1999 shows how the red and orange colours are swept across the roof of the leading driving car in unit 2413. A livery with this arrangement requires regular cleaning using a machine with roof sprays and brushes.

breaks up the visual symmetry and streamlined effect of the cab front, but the overall effect is still excellent. Everything below solebar level is painted black.

The company branding is placed high on the bodyside on the red area above the first and second passenger windows. '**SOUTH WEST**' is in white lettering and 'TRAINS' in the usual orange with a lighter red dot over the capital 'I'. The branding is larger than that on the intermediate coaches, which is itself larger than the form used on suburban EMUs. The unit number is applied as a former SR four-digit number in white rail-alphabet numerals immediately under the driver's cabside window. Individual vehicle numbers are at the right end of the vehicles (left end when the cab is at the right) on the blue band above the bogies.

Fortunately, the design of the Class 159 diesel multiple-units is sufficiently clean to enable this style of painting to transfer across without major change to the livery layout. Those that have so far been repainted in it look very smart indeed.

SOUTH WEST TRAINS

MUM IN A MILLION 1997
DOREEN SCANLON

Above:
SWT continued NSE's policy of naming the buffet cars in the Class 442 EMUs. This is the nameplate on unit 2416.
Brian Morrison

SWT Names
Network SouthEast began the practice of naming the buffet cars on the Class 442 five-car EMUs. SWT has painted names that look like nameplates amidships on the bodysides of the cars.

Above:
Connex applies a standard livery to most of its EMUs and DEMUs, consisting of overall white bodysides with a blue band along the bottom edges, enlivened by yellow decals that fade in stripes to the upper edge and by means of colour grading towards the cab doors. These two Class 319s demonstrate the colours as they pass each other north of South Croydon station on 13 May 1999. No 319 215 (on the left), a refurbished unit working a London-Brighton fast train, has the Connex symbol on its cab front and carries a yellow band above the bodyside windows over the First-class section; No 319 003 is an inner-suburban version without these embellishments. Both are branded '*connex south central*' on each vehicle.

Connex South Central

There was a period of apparent indecision at Connex when the Mk 1 electric multiple-units that ply between London and the South Coast were being repainted following overhaul immediately after privatisation: the company clearly did not wish to continue receiving units in NSE colours, so they were initially painted all-over off-white, with the solebars dark blue. Roofs were dark grey as before, and everything below the solebars was black. Cab ends were warning yellow below windscreen level, and the windscreen surrounds were painted black up to roof level and across the middle of the cab front (including the upper half of the gangway door). Standard OHLE orange warning lines were applied.

Unit numbers were applied in standard white numerals in rail alphabet above both cab windscreens; vehicle numbers were in blue figures on the bodysides in the former standard NSE positions.

The Class 421 and 423 units looked bland for a little while, but the livery mystery was solved when new plastic decals began to be applied to the lower bodysides. These provide a wide strip of yellow along the bodysides, with the upper edge being formed of three yellow stripes with white between them, the yellow and white stripes being graded such that the narrowest yellow and the broadest white are at the top, below the bodyside windows. This gives the visual impression of the yellow merging with the off-white. At the cab end of driving vehicles this is carried a stage further, with the end of the decal terminating in a curve behind the cab door and its colour gradually fading as well, this time by means of breaking the yellow up into progressively finer dots as if in a printing screen. These end decals do not always match exactly the yellow colour of the adjoining decals. At the base of the bodysides is a narrow stripe of dark blue.

The Connex South Central name has not always been applied in full. All units that have the new livery receive the blue spot with its 'twin C' motif that resembles a pair of sharply-curved rails. This is placed on the yellow decals on the lower bodyside. After the blue spot, some units bear the word '*connex*' in sans-serif, bold, dark blue lettering, and

67

Left:
Because on some Class 421 units Connex removed the First-class section from one end of the units, the company wished to emphasise the vehicle in which First class remained. A wider yellow band was painted just above the roof gutter, as seen on unit 1745 on 13 May 1999. Note also the yellow pillars either side of the cab windscreens which carry the figure '1' at the First-class end. The new band on the roof was above the reach of carriage-cleaning machines, and soon became difficult to see. On this unit the narrow yellow band above the windows was still in place. The '*connex*' branding appears on only one vehicle.

Above:
A detail of the livery on a Class 421 unit working in the Connex South Central area shows the blue lining at the base of the bodyside, and also the fact that grab-rails are painted blue. The roof gutter, painted orange, forms the OHLE warning line, which is carried round onto the black vehicle ends using orange tape. On this unit the basic '*connex*' branding permits use of the unit on either South Eastern or South Central services.

others are lettered '*connex south central*'. On modern units such as '319s' and '455s' the branding is on all four coaches, centrally on the intermediate cars and towards the cabs on the outer cars; on units of Mk 1 stock the branding is on only one end coach, towards the inner end. On modern units the unit numbers are placed in full in black as six-digit numbers (unspaced) on the cab fronts below the

driver's side windscreen; older units continue to carry their abbreviated (four-digit) numbers above the windscreens, as in BR days.

An addition to the standard livery was applied to certain Mk 1 units in early 1999. To make the position of the remaining First-class section more visible on those units in which one of the former two First-class sections had been downgraded to Standard, a broad band of warning yellow was painted on the roof just above the cantrail over the relevant section. At the same time, the cab front warning yellow was carried up the pillars outside the windscreens up to cantrail level, and the figure '1' applied to each, further to mark the First-class end of the unit. This livery modification has not been entirely successful, because the yellow bars on the roof are out of reach of mechanical carriage-washing machines, and can thus become seriously obscured by dirt. Some of these units retain the former standard yellow stripe above the windows and below the cantrail to denote the position of First class; others do not.

Connex South Eastern

The Connex South Eastern franchise has been managed by the same corporate management team as has South Central, so it is not surprising that the train liveries appear at first glance to be almost identical. The one major variation, apart from the

branding of the trains '*connex south eastern*', arose from the wish to present the relatively new 'Networker' series Classes 365, 465 and 466 units in Connex livery by application of standard decals without considerable repainting. Thus the NSE blue window bands were retained on these units only. As the combination of yellow and blue forms a satisfactorily striking colour contrast, the result is aesthetically pleasing, and in the author's eyes has more impact than the standard yellow and white form of the Connex livery. Readers can judge for themselves by comparing the photographs of a Class 508 in yellow and white with one of a 'Networker' in yellow and blue.

Above:
For some reason the application of Connex livery to the South Eastern Class 508s transferred from Merseyrail leads to a somewhat bland appearance. This may be because the styling of the cab front bears even less visual relationship with the bodysides than on Mk 1 stock of Classes 411, 421 and 423. Unit 508 210, at South Croydon on a Tunbridge Wells service on 13 May 1999, has the '*connex south eastern*' badge and branding between the sliding entrance doors on each coach.

Above right:
Bright colour contrasts resulted from Connex's applying yellow shaded vinyls to the lower bodysides on Networker EMUs, which retained the NSE blue upper panels because they were not due for repainting. However the, NSE red band above the windows was similarly obliterated by white. Note that the blue panel near the cab end is also a vinyl, to achieve the fading required. No 465 007 approaches Bromley South on 12 July 1999 with the 15.35 service from Sevenoaks to London Blackfriars. This unit still carries the NSE 'lozenge' tricolour symbol below the windscreen.

Right:
A detail of the livery and branding on the side of unit 465 007. Note that, on these units only, the Connex blue band at the base of the bodyside is replaced by the former NSE light grey. The window frames are left unpainted, to smart effect.

4. PARCELS-TRAIN LIVERIES

English, Welsh & Scottish Railway

EWS purchased the BR Rail express systems (Res) at privatisation. Locomotives used to haul parcels trains are gradually receiving the standard EWS maroon livery (see next chapter), whereas parcels vans have thus far remained in the former Res red and black style. This is a former BR livery, described in *Railway Liveries: BR Traction 1948-1995.*

Royal Mail

The first new trains to be accepted for operation on Railtrack lines under the new-vehicle acceptance process set out in Railway Group Standards were the Class 325 electric multiple-units purchased by Royal Mail, though operated by EWS. These four-car units were painted in 'Royal Mail red' — a shade that is reportedly slightly darker than the colour used on road mail vans, to compensate for the greater area of red presented on the side of a train. The red covers the bodysides up to the roof line above cantrail level, cab roof dome, and driving vehicle front farings. The cab windscreens have black surrounds including a wide black panel below the windscreen on which the builder's logo '**ABB**' appears on the left in white, the unit number being displayed under the driver's windscreen in stylish numerals with serifs. Roofs are dark grey and all other items under the floor are black.

Bodyside lining is a bolder version of the yellow stripes used by BR for its early Parcels Sector livery, the two yellow bands continuing along the length of a four-car unit but being angled back sharply behind the cab door to terminate at cantrail level a couple of metres back from the cab door. In the middle of each bodyside is the Royal Mail insignia including the crown. The 'EIIR' symbol with crown above (ER on the three Scotland-based units) appears at the right end of each bodyside, except that it is always at the end away from the cab on driving vehicles. Directly below the Royal symbol, just above the yellow lining, is the vehicle number in yellow numerals.

Below:
The only parcels-train livery that can be attributed to the privatisation era is that applied to the Royal Mail Class 325 four-car EMUs when they were delivered in 1995. No 325 007 approaches Crewe on 7 July 1999 and demonstrates the simplicity of the red livery with its two yellow lining bands and 'Royal Mail' insignia. Note that the crown and 'EIIR' also appear at one end of each bodyside. Features of the cab front are the large black area surrounding the windscreens, and that the area of warning yellow, while possibly visually acceptable, does not meet Railway Group Standard requirements: the main warning-yellow panel should be at least 1sq m in area, with a minimum dimension of 0.6m, which in this application it is clearly not. To the cab front panel the manufacturer has added 'ABB' — a symbol already made obsolete by the subsequent takeover forming Adtranz. Note also that the OHLE orange warning line correctly runs round the bodyside at a constant height and thus crosses the yellow area above the windscreens.

5. FREIGHT-TRAIN LIVERIES

English, Welsh & Scottish Railway

Because EWS was a subsidiary of the Wisconsin Central Railroad in the USA, there was pressure to replicate that railway's livery on locomotives and wagons owned or leased by EWS. The result pleased many observers. Locomotives are painted overall maroon including the roof areas and cab windscreen surrounds. In addition to the usual warning-yellow colour on the cab front below the windscreen (or on the nose of types such as Class 37), there is a broad gold band (nominally 600mm wide) along the middle of the bodyside, strategically located to complement the design of the locomotive; a narrower band is used on Classes 37, 58 and 73. On the gold band are located the initials '**EWS**' and the locomotive number in maroon Gill Sans Bold lettering and numerals.

Above:
The English, Welsh & Scottish Railway developed its locomotive liveries entirely in-house, without resorting to consultants. The result — an adaptation of the colours used on the parent company's locomotives in the USA — is generally regarded as pleasing. No 37883, at Doncaster on 23 September 1997, illustrates the first version of the livery: the gold band carries lettering in Arial Bold font with the ampersand ('&') included — 'EW&S'. Note that the locomotive number is repeated in maroon on the locomotive front.

(Early repainted locomotives had '**EW&S**' and the numbers in Arial Bold typeface.) On one side of a locomotive the '**EWS**' is on the left and the number on the right; the other side has these the opposite way round. In yellow below the cab window at the right-hand end is the EWS logo of three symbolic heads, the English lion, Welsh dragon and Scottish stag, with the name of the company, '**English Welsh & Scottish Railway**', in yellow Gill Sans Bold beneath it. The locomotive number also appears in full, low-down on the warning yellow panel below the driver's windscreen, in maroon or black Gill Sans. At or near the base of the bodyside is a lining strip of reflective yellow. (This is a carry-over by Wisconsin Central of an American safety practice, being intended to reflect the headlights of road vehicles at unprotected level crossings; in the UK it is acknowledged to be purely decorative.) Handrails are white and grilles, buffer beams, underframes and almost everything below underframe level are painted black.

For the new Class 66 and 67 locomotives, a variation of the standard EWS livery was adopted. Even though the body style of the '66s' is the same as that of the Class 59 locomotives, the gold band was rearranged to look more impressive. The band is high on the bodyside for part of its length, and then switches to low-down (where it adjoins the reflective strip) using a 'Z' layout, looking perhaps like a flash. The '**EWS**' and locomotive number are on the upper part of the flash, though all are the opposite way round on the other side of the locomotive.

Diesel shunting locomotives are painted in the standard EWS style, except that the reflective strip is omitted.

EWS Nameplates

This operator has continued the former BR practice of affixing cast aluminium plates on locomotives. Most plates still use the former BR style, with raised rail alphabet upper- and lower-case lettering on black-painted backgrounds, though those on former Res-liveried locomotives have a thicker lettering style.

Above left:
The EWS badge uses the English lion, Welsh dragon and Scottish stag to define the company's territory. The lettering below is in Gill Sans Extra Bold typeface, and the whole is in the same golden yellow as the bodyside lining band.

Left:
Co-Co diesel-electric No 56115 in EWS maroon passes southbound through Doncaster on 9 March 2000 with an empty coal train. The locomotive has the gold lining band in the standard straight form, with the locomotive number and 'EWS' in maroon Gill Sans. The buffer-beam is black and cab windscreen surround maroon. The bottom yellow band is a reflective decal.

Above:
On Class 66 Co-Cos the gold lining band appears in a visually-effective zig-zag form. No 66035 passes Doncaster on 9 March 2000 with a northbound Channel Tunnel freight train. The yellow buffer-beam carries the cab-front warning yellow to a larger area. The cab-front numerals are black.

Wagons are generally painted overall maroon, with the top edge or other suitable line painted with a narrow yellow stripe. They carry the '**EWS**' lettering in yellow at the centre of the wagon body, with the wagon number and key operating data in a neat, yellow-bordered panel with yellow lettering on a maroon background, at the left end of the wagon.

A few inspection saloons of former passenger stock also carry EWS colours. These have the gold band placed closely beneath the bodyside windows with maroon '**EWS**' or '**EW&S**' at one end in large lettering, as on the locomotives, and the carriage number painted small at the other. Footsteps and handrails are white, and the solebars and everything below are painted black.

The two Class 47 locomotives used for Royal Train duties (No 47798 *Prince William* and No 47799 *Prince Henry*) are painted in a special livery that matches the Royal Train coaches. The overall colour is Royal claret. Halfway down the bodysides is a set of lining that uses the standard EWS colours — a 25mm-wide gold line flanked either side by 50mm maroon bands. This lining runs from cab door to cab door exclusive. The locomotive roofs are executive dark grey and the locomotive number is not displayed on the warning yellow panel. On the right-end cab below the cabside window is the EWS crest in polished aluminium; the Royal Crest — the Crown & Cypher — is displayed at the left end. The aluminium numberplates and nameplates use numerals and letters in Res and BR typefaces.

Freightliner

Freightliner Ltd, a small company originally operating only container trains, has shown itself to be bold in its marketing and in its ability to gain traffic from other sources against strong competition. Its company image is enhanced by an original livery for its locomotives that is unlike any other, past or

Left:
Engineer's inspection saloon No DB999504, seen at Toton on 10 May 2000, carries the earlier form of lettering using Arial Bold font and the full 'EW&S'. An addition to the standard livery is the bright red headstock and buffers. The reflective yellow strip is omitted.

Below:
The two 'Royal' Class 47s are owned by EWS and carry a special livery to match the train they haul. No 47798 *Prince William*, photographed at Wolverton works on 10 October 1997, is in deep claret lined-out in EWS maroon and gold. The OHLE warning line is gold, and the locomotive has raised metal numerals in former BR Res style, together with polished Royal Crown insignia.
Bob Sweet

Freightliner Ltd applies a dark green shade that is set off by wider than normal coverage of the cab in warning yellow. An unusual feature is the reflective vinyl applied to the central bodyside in which the word *'Freightliner'* shines out when illuminated by station or yard lighting after dark. Note that the dot on the *'i'* of *'Freightliner'* is red. No 86602 was photographed at Ipswich on 29 June 1999.

On Freightliner's Class 66 Co-Cos there is an additional reflective yellow strip near the base of the bodyside; otherwise the livery is standard. No 66505 pauses between duties at Doncaster on 9 March 2000.

present. Layouts for the new style were provided by stylists The Art Works.

The base colour is a strong mid-to-dark green (Freightliner green) that covers most of the bodysides and the locomotive roofs and cab domes. Each cab front is wholly painted yellow (Freightliner yellow). The yellow extends round to the cabsides, where the bottom edge terminates against the cab door space, while the back edge of the yellow area is angled forward about 10°. Superimposed on the bodyside is a large decal carrying the company name '*Freightliner*' in bold italic sans-serif letters in yellow, but with the dot over the '*i*' displayed as a red triangle. The lettering is based on Helvetica Bold but has been extensively redrawn. This large decal is reflective, and the green and yellow glow it produces when amid yard lighting at night can be striking. The company name is repeated on the cabsides just below the driver's windows on a small reflective decal of the same colouring and lettering style as the main bodyside decal. The locomotive number appears in larger-than-usual broad numerals in reflective Freightliner green at the base of each cabside as well as on the front at the left side when the observer is looking directly at the cab front.

Direct Rail Services

This company, part of British Nuclear Fuels, owns a number of Class 20 and Class 37 locomotives.

These are painted dark blue with warning yellow cab fronts or nose ends and buffer-beams. Locomotive roofs are dark grey. On the Class 37s the locomotive numbers are in large white numerals, unspaced, high on the bodyside near the right-end cab or radiator grilles. The company logo is '**DRS**' in mid-blue bold, sans-serif lettering, with a pale blue band above and below. Beneath that is a wide pale blue block, the whole being sited behind the left cab or on the engine-room doors. Each cabside also has the '**DRS**' motif, though smaller, with the company name in white on the lower pale blue block. The locomotive number is in black Gill Sans, low on the cab front or nose end on the driver's side.

Below:
Direct Rail Services, a branch of the Atomic Energy Authority and thus the only surviving nationalised railway freight company in the country (!), painted its small fleet of Class 20 and 37 diesel locomotives in an unrelieved dark blue. On Class 37s a large DRS logo in two lighter shades of blue appears on the bodyside, at the opposite end from the locomotive number, which is in white. On each cabside is a smaller logo with the words 'Direct Rail Services' added to the lowest blue panel, in white upper- and lower-case lettering. No 37611 was being started-up at Derby on the morning of 4 March 1999.

Foster Yeoman

Although the Foster Yeoman and ARC fleets existed and operated on BR tracks before the railways were privatised and were never part of the BR national fleet, to omit them from this book would be to deny them their place in British railway history as independent train owners. Foster Yeoman Class 59s and their associated bogie bulk-stone wagons had two livery styles in the short period before Foster Yeoman was linked to Mendip Rail. The original style for Class 59 diesel locomotives was all-over silver-grey with two longitudinal blue stripes, as seen in the illustration. The company name '**YEOMAN**' was on the upper stripe in white block capitals, and the locomotive number was on a black-background aluminium plate under the left-end cabside window. The plate at the right end of the bodyside carried the locomotive name. The company symbol, a large blue '**y**' on a white square background, was applied full-body-height alongside the radiator grille. The cab front had the warning-yellow panel below the windscreens including the buffer beam, and the windscreen surround was white. The lower blue lining band was brought across the front, bisecting the warning panel.

Wagons were painted silver-grey, and either had the company name and symbols on attached plates, or the company name was transferred on the bodyside in white lettering on a blue panel. The illustration shows both varieties.

A change in livery in 1998 continued the use of silver-grey, but with a broad blue band along the bodyside of the locomotive and wagons, crossing the front of the cab on the locomotives, on which the warning-yellow colour was confined to the buffer-beam. The blue '**y**' on a white square background was applied as before, but with the addition below of the company name in white on a blue background.

One Yeoman-owned locomotive, No 59003, has been leased to work a related company's services in Germany, for which it has received a unique livery of red and blue, as illustrated. The Yeoman motif on the red band and the DB (German Railways) symbol on the blue are applied corner-to-corner. Nameplates are backed in blue and the roof is white. There is no warning yellow panel.

Below:
Already privately owned when BR was privatised, the Foster Yeoman trains presented a unified appearance, with the silver-grey colour used on both locomotives and wagons. The locomotives were lined-out in dark blue, as seen on No 59005 passing West Ealing on 6 August 1992 on an empty working from Crawley to Merehead. The locomotive carries the large Yeoman '**y**' on its bodyside and the company name '**YEOMAN**' in white on the upper lining band. The wagons carry the '**YEOMAN**' inscription in white on a dark blue panel. *Hugh Ballantyne*

ARC

Attractively painted in a bright yellow, the ARC trains were distinctive. There was a silver-grey band painted right around the locomotives, and the roofs were also silver. Wagons were all-over yellow. The ARC motif midway along the locomotive sides was in specially-designed, large blue block lettering on the yellow area.

Left:
In 1998 the Yeoman company applied its first new livery of the 'privatisation' era, using the dark blue band to blend the locomotives and wagons more completely. Note the totally-revised treatment of the cab front of No 59001, seen at Merehead Quarry on 27 June 1998. The large 'y' was applied in white on a blue panel, with the word 'YEOMAN' incorporated below, and appeared in the same form on locomotives and wagons. *Hugh Ballantyne*

Below left:
Yeoman-owned locomotive No 59003 received a unique livery of red and blue when it was leased to work a related company's services in Germany. Note the Yeoman motif and the German Railways' 'DB' symbol placed together. The warning yellow panel is omitted, as seen at Merehead on 30 April 1997 before the locomotive was exported.
Colin J. Marsden

Below:
Another firm working Mendip quarries was ARC, which purchased four Class 59s. These were liveried in silver-grey and yellow, while the associated wagons were yellow overall. The blue 'ARC' emblem appeared on the yellow band on the locomotives, and was much larger when applied to wagons. No 59101 was arriving at Goodrington stone yard from Westbury on 5 September 1998. *Colin J. Marsden*

Mendip Rail

By combining the Yeoman and ARC fleets into one for joint operations, a complete locomotive and train have been made spare for additional traffic. One locomotive, Yeoman No 59002, has been repainted in Mendip Rail green, with a red stripe above a silver-grey one at the bottom of the bodysides. The green and the grey areas are taken round the front of the locomotive, but the red stripe is thinned out to form a narrow red line at the cab front. Only the buffer-beam bears the warning-yellow colour. The roof is grey. Midway along the bodyside on the green area appears the white 'MRL' logo, with 'MENDIP RAIL' underneath in white on the red band. The OHLE warning line is red.

Hanson

The takeover of ARC by Hanson brought yet another new livery to the railway early in 1999. The dominant new colour is white, the locomotives and wagons both also having a wide, dark blue band along the bodyside and wrapped round the cab fronts on the locomotives. The locomotive roofs have a red band along the centre, bleeding over as a short strip at the top of the cab front. Again, the OHLE warning line is red. Only the buffer-beams are yellow. On the bodysides of all vehicles is the Hanson logo in heavy, white upper- and lower-case sans-serif letters, with a red and white noughts-and-crosses emblem adjacent to the 'H' of 'Hanson'. Number- and nameplates have been repainted with red backgrounds.

National Power

The Class 59/2 locomotives purchased by National Power were given a pleasant shade of mid-blue as their base colour, the whole locomotive body receiving this colour, other than a white band at the base which was separated from the blue by a narrow red line with a wider white one adjacent. The OHLE warning line was correctly in orange. On the cab front the warning-yellow area covered everything below the windscreens including the buffer-beam. Wagons were blue, with grey ends, and were also grey below the point where the bodyside turned inwards towards the solebar. The National Power logo, in white and red inside a white circle and with '**National Power**' in white lettering underneath, was placed midway along the bodysides on the blue area. Locomotive numbers and names were on plates with red backgrounds.

The purchase by EWS of National Power's railway interests has led to the fleet of '59/2s' being repainted in standard EWS colours and reallocated to duties elsewhere.

6. INDEPENDENT ROLLING-STOCK OWNERS

Several operators of tour trains and lessors of stock for emergency and special workings have acquired rakes of ex-BR Mk 1 and Mk 2 stock and painted them in former BR liveries such as carmine and cream, lined maroon, chocolate and cream (Western Region-style) and unlined SR carriage-stock green. Two owners are also using Pullman livery, in one case authentically on preserved Pullman carriages, in another on former BR air-conditioned stock but without the Pullman branding.

Because all these are copies of liveries described in *Railway Liveries: BR Steam 1948-1968*, they are not described again in this book, which concentrates on liveries specific to the privatisation era.

Sea Containers Ltd

This company announced its intention to create a complete train hauled by ex-LMS 4-6-2 No 6229 *Duchess of Hamilton* in its streamlined form and painted in maroon livery with gold stripes; the carriages, less than authentically, would also be painted maroon and striped in gold. In reality, the only vehicle to have appeared in these colours at the time of writing is a Class 50 Co-Co diesel-electric locomotive. This has four gold stripes along the bodysides and across the cab window surrounds, the stripes at the top and bottom being wider than the two in between. This pattern follows the layout of the silver stripes on the prewar blue and silver 'Coronation Scot' set. The warning-yellow panel on

Above left:
Sea Containers Ltd painted Class 50 Co-Co No 50017 in this pseudo-LMS streamliner livery for working special passenger trains. It is seen passing through Stafford, running light-engine from Wolverton to Crewe, on 11 September 2000. *Bob Sweet*

Left:
During its brief period of operations, Waterman Railways painted its locomotives black with LNWR-style red, cream and grey lining. Devoid of any ownership markings, Class 47 Co-Co No 47712 leaves Derby on 23 March 2000 with the 06.40 Virgin CrossCountry train from York to Bristol. Note the red buffer-beam, and that the lining is just one large panel around the bodyside between the cab doors. Much of the Waterman stock has been taken over by Riviera Trains.

the cab front is below the windscreen and the gold stripes.

Waterman Railways

Waterman Railways was a short-lived venture to break into the special train market with a mixture of air-conditioned and conventional rolling stock of Mk 1 and Mk 2 types. The carriages were painted a dark plum similar to the dark claret of the Royal Train, but with off-white lining along the bodyside, just below the side windows. One Mk 2d coach was outshopped with this line higher than the others, and was never corrected. Not all carriages were repainted before the venture ceased to trade.

A different livery was applied to certain Mk 1 coaches, namely a copy of the LNWR off-white and plum. The latest version has off-white panels lined out in black-and-cream giving a quality look to the style.

Locomotives to carry the house livery were Class 47s and a pair of '20s', painted in LNWR lined black, the lining being the red, cream and grey with which observers became familiar as part of the lined black style adopted by BR in 1949 for mixed-traffic steam locomotives. The '47s' had the warning yellow restricted to below the cab front windscreens, and carried the orange OHLE warning line correctly.

Porterbrook Leasing

The Porterbrook Leasing corporate livery is wildly unusual, not only in employing non-traditional colours but also in arraying them in a novel manner. The key colours are pale purple and white, the purple being at one end of the vehicle and linked to the white by two curved bands that sweep from the bottom of the bodyside to cantrail level. The company logo is displayed in purple above the word 'PORTERBROOK'. Running information is in white rail alphabet at the purple end of the vehicle. The style has been used for two Class 47 locomotives and a number of former BG vans that were converted for use as barrier/translator vehicles.

A Class 55 'Deltic' has also received the Porterbrook colours, though in a more traditional layout. Where the production 'Deltics' were originally painted Brunswick green (see *Railway Liveries:*

BR Traction 1948-1995), the Porterbrook locomotive is purple, and it has an off-white band along the lower bodyside as well as white cab window surrounds.

Fragonset

This small leasing company aims at a niche market for spot-leasing of locomotives to meet temporary shortages being experienced by train operators, and for working special trains. The locomotives that have received the standard Fragonset livery are of Classes 31, 33 and 47. The livery is black, with a maroon band along the middle of the bodyside, the band being neatly edged with a fine golden-yellow line. There is a warning-yellow panel below the windscreens, and the buffer-beams are painted red. The overall effect is professional, and is able to combine aesthetically with the livery of virtually any carriage to which a locomotive may be coupled.

Fragonset has a neat circular emblem that is applied to the right-hand cabside. The locomotive number appears on the left-end cabside below the side window, but above (rather than in line with) the level of the bodyside lining band.

The Royal Scotsman

This company paints its carriages in an attractive maroon livery that is lined-out with gold panels. Each carriage carries the name 'THE ROYAL SCOTSMAN' in elongated serif shaded gold lettering. The company crest is carried on the lower

bodysides under the fixed passenger window nearest each end. Carriage roofs are silver-grey, and the maroon colour is carried round the body ends. EWS Class 37 locomotive No 37428 is painted in a

Above:
This view of the 'Royal Scotsman' luxury train on 24 June 1994 illustrates well the use of shadowed lettering, crests and yellow lining to imbue a sense of quality. Note the designation of some of these vehicles as 'State Cars', as identified above the bodyside windows. *Colin J. Marsden*

Left:
Riviera Trains uses a livery of dark blue and cream, lined-out in gold, for its tourist carriages. This livery was observed on a special working at Blaenau Ffestiniog on 9 September 1998. *Brian Morrison*

matching style but with maroon roof. This locomotive carries the Royal Scotsman crest high on the bodyside at the opposite end from the large-sized locomotive number (applied in cream); the EWS crest appears on the right-end cabside in its normal position.

Riviera Trains

Coaches operated by Riviera Trains have a livery of cream and dark blue, the cream being the main window band and the blue covering the lower bodysides and a band above the windows up to the cantrail. They are lined out in gold and the carriage names are on the lower bodysides in dark blue serif capitals on cream panels. There is also a train set in former BR (WR) brown and cream livery.

Eurotunnel

For its fleet of Bo-Bo-Bo electric locomotives Eurotunnel chose to continue the use of grey that had become common throughout Britain's railways during the late-BR era. The style adopted was a three-tone grey. As the locomotives never operate on Railtrack lines there is no requirement for a warning yellow panel, and the space on the cab front where this would normally be is off-white — a colour that is repeated on the bodyside. At the sides of the cab front are dark grey parallel bands that run upwards and over to form the roof colour along the top of the bodysides. Below this, running parallel along each bodyside, is a narrow blue lining band adjacent to a green one. These bands stretch back and upwards from behind the driver's cab door to the back of the locomotive. The cabside itself is largely covered by a wide, mid-grey band angled upwards to the rear and parallel to the dark grey cab-corner band. About one third the way along the bodyside begins another mid-grey area, bounded by a long curve towards and eventually adjoining the green lining band.

The locomotive number is displayed in black on the cab side just below the driver's window, the set of four numerals being bounded by a thin black border. Eurotunnel's circular emblem appears on the forward part of the right-hand cabside. In the centre of the off-white bodyside area is the 'le Shuttle' motif in green italic sans-serif lettering set over an elongated dark blue tick or flash. However, Eurotunnel has now abandoned the use of this name for its services, so the motif can be expected either to disappear altogether or be replaced with something else.

The Eurotunnel car-carrying and lorry-shuttle unit trains are largely of unpainted stainless steel, with a dark blue and green band along the middle of the bodysides.

Below:
The Bo-Bo-Bo electric locomotives of Eurotunnel Ltd that top-and-tail the heavy shuttle trains for road vehicles using the Channel Tunnel have a distinctive livery of shades of grey and white with green and blue lining. The lining bands are carried on along the hauled rolling stock. No 9006 arrives from France at the UK terminal at Cheriton on 6 September 1996. *Hugh Ballantyne*

7. 'SECOND TIME ROUND' PASSENGER LIVERIES

Having settled on corporate liveries for their existing trains, the operating companies that subsequently received newly-built trains reacted in three different ways:

1. Some adapted their corporate liveries to the new vehicles with only minor or cosmetic change; this was the approach adopted by EWS and Freightliner.

2. A number used their existing colours but with changes that significantly altered the vehicles' appearance; examples are South West Trains, with its Class 458 units, and the Class 333 sets in West Yorkshire.

3. Most appear to have decided on a complete change; these include Gatwick Express, First North Western and LTS Rail.

Other changes can be expected as holders of franchises change. For example, Arriva now controls Northern Spirit, and the re-franchising process will introduce further changes, such as GoVia's takeover of the South Central TOC from Connex.

Gatwick Express

The new Gatwick Express Class 460 'Juniper' eight-car units from Alstom make a strong impression from two aspects: they have a sharply-aggressive, streamlined cab-front design, and a much gentler but attractive bodyside livery that exudes comfort and quality. There is in fact no carry-over at all from the livery of the original Gatwick Express trains described in Chapter 1. The new style owes everything to stylists Jones Garrard.

The cab front has a confined but adequate warning-yellow panel below the windscreens. The windscreens have a narrow band of yellow above them that carries up on to the front of the cab roof, and a white band just below. Either side of the cab front is a rakish bright red area, which, when viewed from the side, takes a crudely straight angle up from the cab base to hit the roof line just behind the cab door where it meets the red carriage roof. At the base of the cab, the red area continues across the lower front over the moulding that covers the position of the obstacle-deflector.

The vehicle bodysides are off-white, with a dark grey band along the base. The passenger entrance doors are light grey with a wide pale blue band across the bottom to aid the partially-sighted. On each driving car the word '**EXPRESS**' is placed below the windows in mid-grey bold lettering. The unit number, with the class number spaced out from the unit running number BR-style, is placed low on the dark grey area of the bodyside behind the cab door. The vehicle numbers are also on the dark grey band, but higher up and at the opposite end of the vehicles. Enhanced by dark ribbon-glazing, the side view of these units is impressive and welcoming. One still wonders about the cab ends, however, particularly their somewhat aggressive shape, and the relative insensitivity of the shaping of the red areas.

Anglia Railways

In contrast to Gatwick Express, when Anglia Railways introduced its new multiple-units, this time of Class 170, it adapted its already-successful turquoise to continue as the dominant colour. The

Above left:

The rakish look of the Alstom 'Juniper' Class 460 Gatwick Express EMU comes from its aggressive front-end shape — a shape exaggerated by the angle of the bright red cab-front surround. Seen from the side, this forms a straight edge between the red and the white of the bodyside. The roofs of the carriages are also red. Below the white bodyside colour is a band of grey, and the entrance doors are light grey, with pale blue across the bottom to aid the partially-sighted. The word '*EXPRESS*' is emblazoned very large on the lower bodysides of the end vehicles, and the last two digits of the set number appear below the driver's windscreen. Below and on the opposite side of the warning yellow front is a stylised rendering of '*GATWICK EXPRESS*' in small lettering, similar to that on some of the side windows. The carriage sides have a quality look about them; one is entitled to differing views about the unit ends.

Left:

Anglia Railways applied shaded vinyls as part of the new livery for its Adtranz-built Class 170 DMUs. The turquoise is the colour used in the painted version of the livery on older stock, and is carried over the cab roof and also onto the front spoiler. Note the different treatment of the passenger entrance doors, using white and grey colours to comply with the requirements for partially-sighted people. The use of dark glass and ribbon-glazing adds to the appearance of modernity of the train. No 170 203 was resting at its home depot of Norwich Crown Point on 9 September 1999.

units are in fact off-white overall, offset by dark ribbon-glazing. The turquoise area is applied below the bodyside windows as plastic decals, shaded towards the top so that the turquoise appears to fade out and blend with the white above. At the cab ends the turquoise area is curved and blended to fade out just at the cab front bottom corner. The carriage roofs are a conventional dark grey. The cab fronts have warning yellow in the same positions as all other Adtranz 'Turbostar' and 'Electrostar' units, ie above and below the black windscreen surrounds and shaped in accordance with the front-end physical design. Passenger access doors are painted white down to base level to aid the partially-sighted, though there is mid-grey at the level of the adjacent ribbon-glazing to afford visual continuity. Immediately adjacent to either side of each doorway there is a vertical narrow white band on the bodyside.

The '**Anglia**' company insignia is the same as described in Chapter 1, and is placed midway along each bodyside below the windows, on the turquoise area. The unit number, properly spaced-out, is on the cab front below the driver's windscreen in black rail alphabet; carriage numbers are in black below the end passenger windows. The obstacle-deflector cover is turquoise. This is undoubtedly an attractive and effective livery.

Above:

South West Trains was another recipient of 'Juniper' trains, in the form of outer-suburban Class 458 units. These carry the later livery of Stagecoach colours, with a flare over the cabside similar to that on Class 442s but which terminates on reaching the edge of the roof, painted dark blue. The entrance doors are red, which tends to break up the otherwise harmonious look of the train, as seen on this pair of units leaving Wimbledon on their first revenue-earning trip, the 11.48 service from London Waterloo to Alton on 25 February 2000. *Brian Morrison*

Central Trains

To meet the requirements of the disability regulations, the Central Trains company is modifying its Centro-liveried units slightly to make the doorways stand out visually. Each side of the doorway the Centro green window band is broken by a vertical stripe of light grey.

ScotRail Railways

When Strathclyde PTE supported the purchase of a fleet of Alstom 'Juniper' Class 334 EMUs for services radiating out of Glasgow, it kept the crimson-and-cream colours described in Chapter 2, but with modifications. Chief among these was an increase in the depth of the cream area on the vehicle bodysides,

Above:
**The same style is applied to SWT's new 'Turbostar' DMUs;
with their neater front-end design and greater (23m)
vehicle length, the effect of the livery is less fussy.
No 170 301 arrives at Salisbury on its first crew-training
run on 8 November 2000.** *Colin J. Marsden*

the cream being swept up from the corner of the cab.
A light blue lining band also sweeps up from the
same point and runs below the bodyside windows.
There is no repetition of the former BR black and
gold lining used on the other Strathclyde trains. The
cab front has the crimson colour carried up the
pillars either side of the windscreens and swept back
to form a broad red band above cantrail level. The
rest of the cab front is warning yellow. In addition to
the standard '*SPT*' symbol on each vehicle, the
centre vehicle of a three-car set has the name
'*STRATHCLYDE PASSENGER TRANSPORT*' on
the red band below the windows in large golden-
yellow, bold italic non-serif lettering. The unit
number is on the warning yellow panel below the
driver's windscreen.

South West Trains

When it took delivery of the first Class 458 'Juniper'
EMUs from Alstom, having already established two

quite different liveries utilising the basic Stagecoach
house colours, South West Trains decided to adapt
the flashier style used on the Class 442 and 159
units. There are, however, two key differences.
Firstly, the passenger entrance sliding plug doors are
not at the vehicle ends, yet are still painted bright
red overall; this meets the requirements of disability
regulations but wrecks the visual line of the trains,
just as the silver-grey doors do on the Class 333
units at Northern Spirit. The second key difference is
that the carriage roofs are painted dark blue instead
of white. The cab front is almost entirely warning
yellow, with only narrow black surrounds to the cab
windscreens. This livery style has carried across
quite well, but with a white roof, to the new
Class 170s put into service by SWT during 2000.

First North Western

For its new Class 175 DMUs, First North Western
applied to its trains the colours of its holding
company, FirstGroup. The latter's policy has been to
use its corporate colours only on modern road
vehicles that are environmentally friendly, and this
philosophy has now been extended to rail. The base
colour is dark ('reflex') blue. Below and almost
adjacent to the bodyside windows there is a pink
('rubine red') lining band next to a wider white one.
These bands extend between the passenger access

doorways, and also continue beyond them to the non-cab vehicle ends. Above the bodyside windows is a narrow pink line. Both pink lines extend across the passenger access doors at the non-cab ends of the units. The pink and white lining is broken at the middle of the vehicle by a shaded blue area displaying '**North Western**' in white, bold sans-serif lettering. The FirstGroup emblem is placed in a large size in pink at bodyside window level alongside each passenger doorway.

The more dramatic part of the livery is the treatment of the cab end of the bodyside. Starting from a point at the cab front marker lamp holder are pink and white lines together, blue above and then a white area bordered by the warning yellow of the cab front. The pink line sweeps up and across the cab door and levels out with its top at about cantrail level. However, the line then fades out into white about one third along the vehicle. The blue area that is part of the cabside sweep widens and then shrinks to nothing at the top of the cab door. Passenger access doors are white overall, with a decal fading to pale blue at the foot of the door but with a white line each side. The FirstGroup emblem appears on the leading door: '**First**' in blue and the '*f*' logo in pink. Note that the 'i' in '**First**' is not dotted.

The cab front is warning yellow with narrow black windscreen surround and a white band extending across above the head and marker lamps. Below the lamps the cab front including faring is dark blue. The roof line appears to be white when viewed from below, but the centre part of the roof is actually black. This black is carried over the cab roof dome to meet the warning yellow at the OHLE orange warning line. Below the bodyside the underframe farings between the bogies, the bogies themselves and other equipment are painted black.

This is quite a difficult livery to describe, and that may be a commentary in itself, as the style has an odd mixture of straight lining and sharply sweeping curves that do little to blend with the form of the vehicle itself. This author feels uncomfortable with the overall effect.

The Greater Manchester PTE-liveried trains have now received branding indicating the presence of FirstGroup. The '**First**' emblem appears in plain white on the lower bodyside in the dark grey area close to the cab door. The 'North Western' is inboard of it, in smaller, standard lettering.

First Great Western

The colours used for the new Alstom 'Coradia' Class 180 DMUs for First Great Western are the same as for First North Western Class 175s, with the following exceptions.

Instead of a white lining band below the pink band beneath the bodyside windows there is a gold band, similar to that on the green and cream FGW HSTs. As on the '175s', this lining band is faded out for a short length in the middle of each coach, to make way in this case for the name 'Great Western', which is also in gold. The pink band now runs across the base of the cab front, below which is the '**First**' logo in gold. Also, the warning-yellow colour fades out into the white as it sweeps back towards the roof.

LTS Rail / c2c

LTS Rail is unique in that the new trains it ordered and placed into service during the term of the first franchise period have appeared in two successive liveries, each quite different. The first livery, of white with dark green, was the style ordered with the new 'Electrostar' units built by Adtranz. However, the decision to upgrade the image of the railway with the new marketing brand 'c2c' led to one unit's being demonstrated in relatively plain purple — a colour that is intended at the time of writing to be extended to the other units in the fleet.

The original style was off-white overall on the bodysides and cab front, including the cab roof dome. Dark green was used as a band across the bottom of the bodysides and ends and also picked out the entrance doors. The carriage roofs were painted light grey. No 'LTS' branding was applied, because the 'c2c' decision had already been made before the first Class 357 units were put into service. One pair of doors on one vehicle in each four-car set was painted with a broad lime-green band across the middle to denote the wheelchair access point. The unit number was fixed in black rail alphabet below the cab windscreen on the warning-yellow panel. The yellow areas are exactly the same as on the same manufacturer's 'Turbostar' diesel units previously described.

The c2c livery is plain mid-purple with an excess of white in the pigment which tones down its brightness. There is a darker purple band at the base of the bodysides. Entrance doors are light grey. The cab front, apart from the standard 'Electrostar'/'Turbostar' warning panel, is all-purple. The 'c2c' logo, in red figures and letters bordered in white, is placed midway along each bodyside, below the windows.

WAGN — Stansted Express

A complete change was justified by West Anglia Great Northern when the company re-launched its Stansted Express service to and from Liverpool Street in the summer of 2000, using substantially-refurbished Class 317 EMUs. These were painted bright blue overall, including the roofs, with the blue extending across the top of the cab front above the gangway connection. Passenger entrance doors are silver-grey. The cab front, including the windscreen surrounds, is all-over warning yellow. The branding 'stansted express' appears in red midway along the bodysides, below the centre passenger windows. Above the windows of the First-class section are the words 'Business Class' in white. The livery looks smart, if somewhat unoriginal, but has no obvious visual connection with the trains that operate the company's other services.

Virgin Trains

The new 'Pendolino' and 'Voyager' units, on which Virgin Trains has pinned its future, have a common livery. Carriage sides are silver-grey. Black side-

Left:
The new FirstGroup style for Great Western units of Class 180 is very similar to that for First North Western Class 175s, but uses the gold band that is a characteristic of the second version of the GWT green and white style. On No 180 101 the unit number is in dark blue on a small yellow panel low on the cab front. The set was seen on the test track at Old Dalby on 18 April 2000. *Tony Miles*

Below left:
Introduced into service nearly two years after construction, the first LTS Rail 'Electrostar' Class 357 EMUs had a simple livery of white with a dark green band along the base of the bodysides and which covered the overrider pods below the cab front. The passenger entrance doors were dark green to make them easily visible. The cab-front treatment was the same as on Adtranz's 'Turbostar' DMUs. Because the LTS service was re-launched in the summer of 2000 as 'c2c', complete with a new livery, no company branding appeared on trains in the white and green livery. No 357 014 passes Shadwell on the 10.30 London Liverpool Street-Shoeburyness service on 13 October 2000.

Below:
The livery branded 'c2c' is all-purple apart from grey entrance doors. There is a darker shade of purple along the base of the bodysides. Unit 357 025 carries the new livery at the Adtranz works at Derby on 29 June 2000. *Tony Miles*

Above left:
At London Liverpool Street on 22 August 2000 — launch-day of the newly-branded WAGN service to Stansted Airport — unit 317 708 demonstrates the new Stansted Express style: plain blue overall with darker blue doorway surrounds that run up and over the roof, and silver-grey passenger doors. Window frames are left unpainted to break up the bodyside colour. *Brian Morrison*

Left:
This detail of unit 317 708 shows the 'stansted express' lettering and the 'Business Class' labelling above the windows. Note the colour of the doorways.
Colin J. Marsden

Above:
The colours for Virgin's new high-speed trains — the Alstom 'Pendolino' units and the Bombardier 'Voyagers' — are grey bodysides with red roofs and cabsides, black around the windows, with reflective diagonal-hatched doorways. This early 'Voyager' unit was photographed at Bruges in Belgium on 6 December 2000 when on a press-demonstration run to Ostend. *Brian Morrison*

window surrounds are confined to the bodyside windows area only. Each cab end is surrounded by a bright red area that sweeps up and back behind the driver's door to merge with the red vehicle roof. A narrow white stripe separates the red and silver-grey areas. The cab front has a black area curved round the single windscreen, then sweeping up over the cab roof and terminating across the roof behind the cab. The yellow warning area, viewed from the front, forms a broad 'U' shape between the black and red. The upper legs of the 'U' run back along the edges of the black cab roof and join in a band across the roof behind the cab, separating the red and black roof areas.

Passenger entrance doors are hatched in black and white reflective diagonals. The 'Virgin' emblem appears in red on the grey expanse on the end car bodyside between the cab and the first passenger entrance door.

8. FUTURE PROSPECTS

So, when will the new post-privatisation liveries finally settle down, and all trains be painted in their new colours? Unfortunately, it is not as simple as that. It is educational to list those former BR train operators which (at the time of writing, in early 2001 — four to five years after privatisation) have completed their initial repainting programmes (ignoring shunting locomotives, advertising liveries, and any subsequent reallocation of vehicles between TOCs), and then those that have not, and which therefore are still running with BR-liveried vehicles in their fleets.

Repainting complete	Repainting partially complete	Repainting not started
Gatwick Express	Anglia Railways	Chiltern Railways *
First Great Western	Virgin West Coast	
Great North Eastern Railway	Virgin CrossCountry	
Midland Mainline	First North Western	
Merseyrail Electrics	Northern Spirit	
First Great Eastern	Central Trains	* New trains are, however,
Thameslink	Wales & West	in new livery.
Island Line	Cardiff Railways	
	LTS Rail	
	WAGN	
	Silverlink	
	South West Trains	
	Connex South Central	
	Connex South Eastern	
	ScotRail	
	Thames Trains	
	EWS	
	Freightliner	
Total 8	**Total 18**	**Total 1**

Above left:
DMU No 165 110, left, arriving at Reading on the 12.28 service from London Paddington to Bedwyn on 12 April 1999, not only still carries Network SouthEast colours and branding but also has no sign of its Thames Trains ownership. In contrast, the South West Trains Class 423 unit at Platform 4, waiting to leave for Waterloo, has been fully re-liveried.

Left:
As privatisation spread and train-operating companies began the task of repainting their stock in new liveries, we were once again presented with 'piebald' trains (ie with carriages and locomotives carrying differing liveries). An example is this Virgin HST approaching New Milton on 12 June 1999 while working the 11.20 'Dorset Scot' from Bournemouth to Edinburgh. Will we see this sort of thing yet again in the future, now that re-franchising is on its way?

Thus less than a third of all the operating companies that emerged from BR's privatisation have succeeded in achieving traction and rolling-stock fleets wholly in their own colours. The majority still have some vehicles in one or other of British Rail's former business colours. Three or four have hardly started. How soon will these old liveries disappear?

Virgin is well advanced in livery replacement, even though its policy has been to repaint only when this would normally be due. If all goes to plan, the arrival of its new fleets of 'Pendolinos' and 'Voyagers' will displace in the next couple of years those locomotives and Mk 2 carriages that remain in BR livery. Anglia Railways, whose former InterCity trains are already fully branded, has started repainting its ex-BR DMU fleet, though it may lose these units in a forthcoming franchise boundary reshuffle.

Above:
Will the new owner of the Merseyrail Electrics franchise want to change the excellent colours of the existing trains? On 15 May 1999, unit 507 011 arrives at Brunswick *en route* from Hunt's Cross to Southport.

First North Western and Northern Spirit look like being transformed by another franchise rearrangement, so neither may exist in the future, though repainting in existing franchise colours is likely to continue at least until Arriva comes up with a new livery for its newly-acquired interest in Northern Spirit.

Central Trains, Wales & West and WAGN are all in the melting-pot as concerns future franchise boundaries and ownership. The future of South West Trains' liveries depends on Stagecoach's retaining the franchise. GoVia, taking over the South Central franchise, will doubtless quickly eradicate the Connex style — actually quite easy when most of its trains are to be replaced with new ones and the rest are already liveried with decals. A pictorial preview suggests a white livery with strong Southern Railway olive-green decoration, as befits what may emerge as the New Southern Railway. Connex South Eastern looks more secure, as it is a longer franchise. Silverlink and Thames Trains may change significantly in the process, although they have not refrained from full-scale repainting. If First Great Eastern takes over the local services from Anglia and absorbs part of WAGN, it will need to extend its

colours to these trains. The energy it showed in branding its present fleet suggests it may well do that quickly, too, subject to the usual considerations about retaining the franchise.

Merseyrail Electrics and Island Line could find themselves with different owners, but one could accept that the liveries in those cases need not change, save that dinosaurs may not be considered appropriate for Island Line's future rolling-stock replacements! Merseyrail has, however, begun to paint out the black lining band on its EMUs, as mentioned in Chapter 2.

We can thus expect to continue in a world of multiple-liveried trains for many years to come. It may be appropriate now to suggest that the publisher consider another book in this series in three years' time: *Railway Liveries: Post-Privatisation 2001-2003*!

9. HOW IS IT DONE?

In this chapter the author takes the reader through the vastly differing processes of livery design that have been used by those companies which have achieved what, in many observers' eyes, are successful livery applications. One company has done this using its own internal resources; most have used the services of professional stylists to bring greater originality.

English, Welsh & Scottish Railway

This was fully an in-house livery as dictated by the holding company, Wisconsin Central. Engineers based at Toton depot were told to investigate how the Wisconsin corporate colours of maroon with a gold stripe, which looked fine on tall, single-cab, hood-unit, American diesels, could be applied to traditional

Above:
A satisfactory livery developed entirely in-house by engineers — such is the style on EWS General Motors Co-Co No 66144, posing at Toton depot on 10 May 2000. Can anyone disagree?

full-width (and smaller) British locomotives. (The Wisconsin Central livery was originally taken from that of the Soo Line.)

Initial attempts to adapt the livery involved locomotive diagrams printed out on large (A3) paper sheets, an engineer then using water-colour paints, crayons and colour pens to colour-up the diagrams.

It soon became clear that the overall concept was satisfactory, but that there would be difficulty in

Left:
'Respecting the architecture of the train' is the maxim of stylist Best Impressions, which did just that in designing the sweeping style for South West Trains' Class 442 units. Newly-painted No 2416 stands at London Waterloo on 17 June 1998.

Right:
Does the livery of the Class 175 DMUs for First North Western really respect the shape of the train? No 175 001 was stabled at Kidderminster when photographed on 9 October 1999.

meeting the Chief Executive's early wish that the words 'Wisconsin Central' be emblazoned in red capital letters along the gold band. There were also attempts to fit in the WCRR logo (something like an upside-down Christmas tree) in maroon, in the middle of the warning-yellow panel, but it just looked out of place.

A sample plate painted in Wisconsin Central maroon was flown across from the USA and paint mixed in the UK to match it. Thus there is no BS number or Pantone reference to describe the colour adopted by EWS for its locomotives and rolling stock.

The painting convention adopted was for the bodysides, roofs and ends to be maroon, grilles, buffer-beams, underframes and bogies black, and a reflective yellow tape to be applied along the bottom of the bodysides. The reflective tape is a safety feature taken from Wisconsin Central practice, and arose from the need in the USA for locomotives to be visible at night to motorists approaching the many unguarded road crossings. Only Class 08 shunting locomotives did not receive the reflective strip (because they never speed across level crossings?). The decision to go for maroon lined in gold as the corporate EWS livery was relatively easy to take, but 'the devil was in the detail', as always.

The first 'final' drawing used the letters '**EW&S**' in Arial Bold lettering in maroon on the gold band, spaced about 10% further than would be normal on a word-processor. The locomotive number was also in the same style, the class number and locomotive number being grouped as a single five-figure

number, not spaced-out as BR had formerly insisted. Different positions and widths of the central gold band were used, depending on the shape of the locomotives to which it was applied. Most classes looked fine with a 600mm-wide gold band, but Classes 37, 58 and 73 (the more old-fashioned shapes) looked better with a 550mm band. The lettering was applied in maroon, with a clearance from the edge of the band of about 20mm.

After several locomotives had been so painted, a change was adopted that became the final standard. The lettering and number style was changed from Arial to Gill Sans and the ampersand was omitted, so that the letters read '**EWS**'. The railway initials and the locomotive number were at opposite ends of the gold band on each side, ie on one side the '**EWS**' was at the left and the number on the right; on the other side the reverse applied.

Nameplates would be to former BR corporate-image style (unless a customer or official specified otherwise) and would be placed above the locomotive numbers and any crests above the nameplates. If there was no room for a crest in that position it would go below the gold band. A competition was held among EWS staff and readers of *RAIL* magazine to develop a company logo, from which resulted the popular 'three heads' symbol that displays the English lion, Welsh dragon and Scottish stag, side by side. This was developed by Tom Connell, a designer from Reading.

When new Class 66 and 67 locomotives were ordered, another sample of Wisconsin Central maroon plate was sent to General Motors; this mix of maroon is said to be slightly lighter than the British

mix! There was no problem with the warning-yellow colour because that is defined accurately in a British Standard.

The Work of Best Impressions

Several Train Operating Companies have used the services of independent, specialist 'designers' (or, more accurately, 'stylists') to come up with train liveries that have broken away from the more traditional styles used by British Rail. One such company is Best Impressions, run from London by Ray Stenning, a stylist with considerable flair for innovative livery layouts and colours. It was Best Impressions that launched the Midland Mainline green and tangerine livery on a surprised public, and that later amazed everyone with the confident swathe of bright colours on the SWT Class 442 trains.

Ray Stenning's approach starts with 'respecting the architecture of the train', ie not applying a livery layout in a form that ignores the physical shape and lines of the vehicles that form the whole train. The Midland Mainline treatment for HSTs was painstakingly developed on-site, with a power car set aside for trial applications. Best Impressions does not attempt to design using merely side- and end-elevation drawings of the vehicles: Ray says that he has to work out the livery curves and lines with the train in front of him. Lining is placed on a subject vehicle empirically using masking tape, and repeatedly repositioned until the stylist is satisfied with the flow of the lines. (Stenning said to the author that some TOCs' train liveries look as though they have been simply drawn on a side elevation, with no regard to their three-dimensional effects.)

The author — this is not necessarily Ray Stenning's view — sees the First Great Western HST style as following this pattern; surprisingly, the Jones Garrard treatment of the Gatwick Express Class 460 aggressive front end shape also looks as though it came directly off a side-view drawing, so angular is the red stripe's side elevation.)

As far as the development of the Midland Mainline HST style is concerned, the use of stripes was a deliberate throwback to the LMS 'streamliner' striped liveries used in particular on the 'Coronation Scot' train, though in this case placed below the bodyside windows. Indeed, one scheme suggested was of maroon coaches with tangerine stripes — a style that would have delighted Midland Railway enthusiasts, no doubt. However, the spectrally-opposite colour of green was chosen as being a complete break from the past. The shade is known, in railway circles only, as 'teal green'. For MML, the lettering style and the 'leaping stag' motif were designed by Saatchi & Saatchi. On the intermediate coaches on a MML HST the smaller 'MIDLAND MAINLINE' lettering was intended always to be on the upper right end of the bodysides, not on the left end as often applied.

The style laid out for the South West Trains Class 442s also used the idea of a colour sweep from below the cab front up the bodysides, and in this case right over the front vehicle roof. The result is splendid, as already described in Chapter 3. On the Class 458 the angle of the sweep-up is sharper than on the '442s' and '159s', and the roof is dark blue instead of white owing to the absence of roof-cleaning equipment at strategic points in the new units' intended area of operation.

What might have been! A mature proposal for the Central Trains livery for Class 158 DMUs was developed by Best Impressions. In this the blue/green divide was to follow the natural shape of the cabside windows and sweep over the bodyside in a grander curve than that finally adopted. The Central Trains logo of four semi-circles would have appeared full-body-height in white at each end of the unit, with the '**CENTRAL TRAINS**' missive, also in white, above the windows at the inner ends of the carriages. The bright green was carried further over the roof, above the cantrail. Across the bottom of the cab front were the blue and bright green bands, and the spoiler was shown as black. Entrance doors had the yellow area constrained to be in line with the dark grey window band. Regrettably it was not to be!

The Best Impressions philosophy was also applied to good effect in WAGN's livery for its Class 317 suburban units. Indeed, one can list the basic rules that underpin the 'Stenning style':

• Respect the lines/architecture of the train.
• Take up the house colours and lettering of the owning company, if available.
• Use a dark colour across the bodyside windows to create homogeneity.
• Bring the roof into the livery, if possible.
• Put together colours that 'fizz'!
• Use a third colour or lining to 'pull out' other contrasting colours.
• To meet the Disability Discrimination Regulations, entrance doors need to be in a contrasting colour, low-down in the livery: short-sighted people apparently tend to look downwards as they walk.

The point about the use of a third colour to 'pull out' adjacent colours is made by the Central Trains livery, where the blue cab-front area adjoins the bright green, using a red line to separate them. Without the red line, the effect would be satisfactory but far less startling. Ray's words on this to me were: 'The red acts as a catalyst and fires all the colours together.'

Indeed, there are some other useful points illustrated by the Central Trains livery. Some companies pay a stylist to produce their new livery and then change it in detail, thereby reducing its symmetry or impact, probably out of professional ignorance of key design principles. CT's repeated application on the lower bodysides of the 'CENTRAL' symbol and motif, and also the addition of the telephone number on each carriage side, could be said to degrade what is a brilliantly homogenous styling of otherwise humdrum-shaped trains. Another issue is that the Central Trains 'C' logo was expected to be applied as a virtually full-bodyside-height symbol at each end of the dark glazing area (or dark-painted window area on '158s') — this would have been a striking finishing touch.

In the case of the Class 158 style for Central Trains, I understand that another design house finished off the detail of the livery. The sweep of the blue area across the cabside was originally intended to run up at a lesser angle and line up with the angle at the lower back corner of the driver's side window. Instead, the border between the blue and green crosses the window space and thus breaks the Ray Stenning rule about respecting the lines of the train. The illustration above shows what was originally intended; readers can judge for themselves whether the real thing is an improvement or not.

Appendix A: Departmental Vehicle Liveries

Porterbrook Leasing

The Porterbrook livery for locomotives and barrier/translator vehicles was described in Chapter 6. The former BG vans in this livery are used to enable rakes of passenger stock such as HST Mk 3 coaches to be hauled by freight locomotives (such as are owned by EWS) in the absence of their normal power cars; this is usually between depots and works, and results in odd combinations of vehicle liveries, since none of the other companies' styles remotely matches the Porterbrook colours.

Above:
A Porterbrook-liveried barrier/translator vehicle stands at Derby on 12 December 1999, its purple colour having faded to mauve.

Railtrack

In its first three years Railtrack adopted a somewhat downbeat style for rolling stock that performed mundane tasks such as de-icing conductor rails. Most of these vehicles were former electric or diesel multiple-units. At that time Railtrack had embarked upon a corporate style in which shades of gold and brown were used. The departmental vehicles that had been converted from normal carriages were liveried in a light golden-brown colour, with white and grey bands at the bottom of the bodysides. The name '**RAILTRACK**' was applied in brown Gill Sans capitals to the left end of the white band, and the slogan '**CLEARING THE WAY**' applied at the other end of the unit or vehicle. Cab fronts were all-over warning yellow, and all other lettering was black.

A new corporate style emerged in 1999 using dark blue and lime green. Coaching-stock vehicles are now painted with the bodysides in dark blue, but from above the bogie centres a curve of lime green sweeps up to align with the gutter, so that the ends of the bodyside are fully lime green. Lettering on these vehicles is usually placed on the dark blue area in white Gill Sans. An adaptation of this style has been

Above:
The latest Railtrack livery as applied to a Windhoff multi-purpose vehicle stabled at Toton on 10 May 2000, showing how little of the vehicle is actually green or blue. The underframe is black, and the modules carried on the vehicle are grey. The warning-yellow area covers the cab front below windscreen level, the buffer-beam and the obstacle-deflector shield.

applied to the company's Windhoff multi-purpose vehicles (MPVs).

Hunslet-Barclay

In the mid-1990s we became used to seeing former BR Class 20 Bo-Bo diesel-electrics in a plain two-tone grey livery after being purchased by Hunslet-Barclay for main-line departmental duties such as powering weed-killing trains. On these locomotives the running numbers were applied to the cabsides in black.

Merseyrail Electrics

PTE-supported Train Operating Company Merseyrail Electrics operates a number of de-icing vehicles

Left:
Sandite unit No 930 203 carries Railtrack's first standard livery of light brown, white and grey. It is seen heading towards Maidstone at Otford Junction on 1 November 1998. *Hugh Ballantyne*

Left:
DMU 'bubble car' No 977859 (numbered also as unit No 960 011) shows off its new Railtrack green and dark blue colours at Wigan on 2 October 2000. The branding on the blue area is in green and reads: 'RAILTRACK — the heart of the railway — route modernisation with **Balfour Beatty**'.
Tony Miles

Left:
Wagons used exclusively on Railtrack contracts are often now painted dark green, as are these PNA four-wheelers owned by CAIB and numbered 3801 and 3803. Railtrack lettering is in silver-grey. Adjacent vehicles are in EWS colours — maroon with yellow edges. *M. John Stretton*

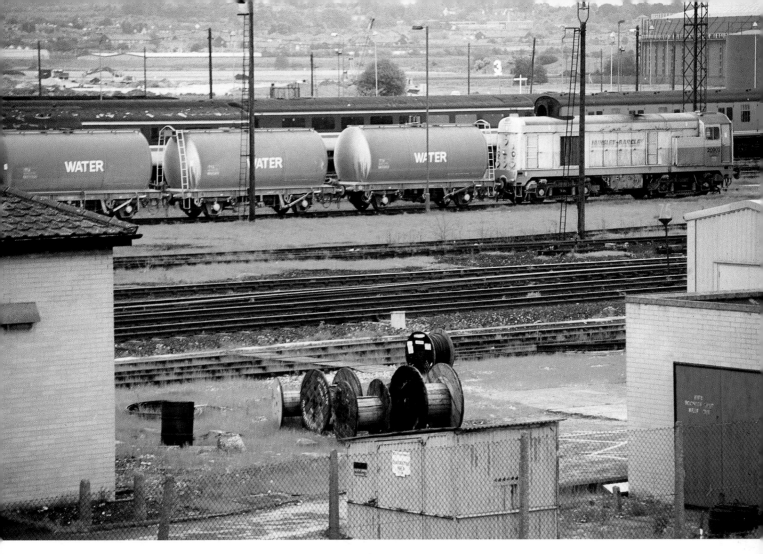

(converted from former Southern Region EMUs), plus a couple of Class 73 Bo-Bo electro-diesels, in overall yellow, with a black band along the bottom edge of the bodysides.

Great North Eastern Railway

A small number of Mk 2 coaches were modified with blanked-out windows and brake-translator equipment for use as barrier vehicles for the movement of individual GNER passenger coaches. These vehicles received the standard GNER colours of midnight blue and red stripe but without the detailed branding. At least one Mk 1 service vehicle has been observed in plain blue, with no lining.

SERCo Railtest

SERCo Railtest, a company that was bought out from the former BR Central Services, owns several laboratory and test coaches. These have been decked out in mid-grey splashed with red with white lettering, as shown in the illustration. The coaches are frequently seen marshalled with either a Railtrack coach in blue and green, or with dark blue AEA Technology Rail laboratory car No 5.

AEA Technology Rail

This company operates a laboratory coach converted from a Mk 2 passenger vehicle. This has been

liveried with dark blue bodysides lined out and lettered in white.

On-track Plant

It has been a long-term practice for on-track machines such as tampers, ballast cleaners and other civil engineering plant to be painted bright yellow, in the same way as much road-repair plant is. Yellow is a very visible colour and is appropriate as a means of warning people of the dangers of moving machinery. In BR days such machinery was usually painted yellow overall, with perhaps a slight respite if the cab roof was painted grey or black, for example. This trend has continued after privatisation and the splitting-up of the former British Rail Infrastructure Services (BRIS) into a number of smallish units that were then sold either to management buy-outs or to large civil-engineering companies such as Balfour Beatty and Amey Plant. The sections that follow illustrate the main exceptions to the all-yellow livery styles.

Jarvis Rail

The Jarvis group developed a maroon livery for its road vehicles which it wanted to transfer across to its rail-mounted machines. The style used is quite simple in that the vehicles are painted maroon overall, with the exception of the forward-facing surfaces at each end of the vehicle, which are painted warning yellow.

Balfour Beatty

Balfour Beatty plant is well-known outside railway circles for its blue and white livery style. The company brought these colours into railway use on its track-maintenance machines, again ensuring that forward-facing surfaces were painted warning yellow.

Amey Rail

Yellow on-track machines operated by Amey Rail that have recently been painted are distinguishable by the short, blue lines with rounded ends that appear on suitable side surfaces, almost as a trademark.

Amec

Another company that operates tamping machines, Amec uses a deep orange to differentiate these from those of other companies. All retain the warning-yellow ends.

Grant Rail

This company operates on-track machinery in a blue and dark yellow livery. Lower bodysides are

mid-blue while above waist level is dark yellow, a
few shades darker than the warning yellow on the
machines' cab fronts. The dark yellow is carried
over the roof or top of the machine. Because the
normal OHLE orange warning line might blend
too closely with the dark yellow colour, the
warning line is white. Below-solebar equipment is
painted warning yellow.

Railtrack-owned heavy rail-borne plant remains in
all-yellow livery, with the initial exception of the
Windhoff multi-purpose vehicles (MPVs). These use
the latest dark blue and lime green style with small
warning yellow panels on the lower cab fronts. Other
Railtrack on-track machines, such as the
stoneblowers and dynamic track-stabilisers, retain

Top:
**At Derby on 3 April 2000 was Amey Rail's tamper
No DR73912, in all-over yellow but with distinguishing blue
stripes with rounded ends, and a blue band across the base
of the machine.**

Above:
**Railtrack continues the use of the traditional yellow colour
on most of its machines, such as stone-blower No DR80206,
seen at Leicester on 31 May 1999.**

their all-over yellow inherited from BR. Breakdown
cranes are still yellow, as described in the previous
book, and independent snowploughs retain their
black with wasp stripes from decades ago.

Appendix B: Experimental and Unofficial Liveries

First North Western

FNW's first essay into its blue livery for middle-aged stock took the form of a plain-blue Class 150. In reality, the blue used was not the shade finally chosen, and the gold stars were omitted.

South West Trains

At a time when its corporate style was under development, SWT, not wanting to repaint an old unit in BR's more elaborate NSE colours, a Class 411 unit was painted locally in a simplified blue and white version following graffiti damage.

When the first Class 458 'Juniper' EMU was first delivered for trial running, it appeared in an overall bodyside white without many markings. True, the warning yellow ends were there, as were the red cab-front surrounds, but the full SWT livery was not applied for many weeks.

Connex

Chapter 3 has already referred to the period when Connex had repainted electric multiple-units delivered from works without the yellow decals on them. Thus the units were painted off-white overall, with blue solebars and dark grey roofs. Although not an official livery, it was the base for the future Connex style, and many units remained thus 'decorated' for many months before finally receiving the full livery.

Below:
Before the North Western Trains livery was finalised, DMU No 150 134 appeared in plain blue of a different shade. The unit was at Manchester Oxford Road *en route* to the Airport station on 17 March 1999. *Tony Miles*

West Anglia Great Northern

WAGN has also had a period when its ability to muster fully-repainted Class 313 and 315 units has been lacking, and many of these have been turned out from works in plain off-white.

Silverlink

When Silverlink was said to be struggling to keep up passenger interest in its service between Bedford and Bletchley, Bletchley depot made a strong attempt to smarten-up the rolling stock used on this short shuttle service. Two Class 121 diesel railcars were repainted, one being in a simplified version of the original Network SouthEast style with the earlier, lighter blue. The other received full Silverlink colours as applied to more modern multiple-units, except that there was no great sweep or wave of the purple and green bodyside colours; the window band was straight dark purple, and below the windows was painted lime green. Only the driver's doors were painted yellow, as having that colour on the array of passenger slam doors would probably have been visually alarming.

Wales & West

Before deciding on the grey and yellow livery described in Chapter 2, Wales & West turned out a Class 158 unit in a more striking style that still used silver-grey as the main body colour, but over a shorter length of about six bodyside windows. The ends of each bodyside are in Royal blue — a colour that contrasts sharply with orange swing plug doors. Between the dark blue and the silver-grey is a vertical band of light blue that is curved towards to cab end, and this is separated from the grey by a narrower orange band. Carriage roofs are dark grey, and the cab front, including the obstacle-deflector, is all-over warning yellow.

Left:
Not wanting to repaint Class 411 unit No 1568, a victim of graffiti, in the old Network SouthEast colours, SWT reached a compromise and the unit appeared uniquely in blue and white. It is seen on 4 September 1996 working the 11.12 London Waterloo-Alton. *Brian Morrison*

Below left:
When the first Class 458 unit was delivered to South West Trains the final livery was still uncertain, and it appeared in plain white except for the treatment of the cabs. Unit 8001 stands at Wimbledon depot on 19 February 1999. *Colin J. Marsden*

Below:
Repainted but still waiting for vinyls, Connex unit 1748 is all-over off-white, but with blue solebars. It is seen near Wateringbury with the 14.20 Maidstone-Three Bridges service on 29 August 1999. *Brian Morrison*

Left:
When the Class 375 EMUs were being built and tested for Connex South Eastern, no livery was applied. No 375 607 stands in Adtranz's works yard at Derby in plain off-white apart from the yellow cab front and black ribbon glazing on 20 July 2000.
Tony Miles

Centre left:
A white Class 313 is not a pretty sight, but a number are running like this. No 313 029 calls at Finsbury Park on 10 April 2000.

Bottom left:
Silverlink applied this special livery to single car No 55027, labelled as unit 121 027 and seen at Bletchley on 3 February 1999. The vehicle was at the rear of the 16.50 to Bedford.

Above right:
The experimental livery applied to Wales & West's unit No 158 867 for the 'Alphaline' services was considerably more colourful than the version finally adopted. The unit approaches Dawlish Warren on 4 March 2000 with the 06.15 from Penzance to Manchester Piccadilly.
Colin J. Marsden

Right:
Virgin Trains painted this Class 86, No 86245 *Caledonian*, in a blue livery with maroon stripes, spaced out wider than the white stripes on other Virgin stock. The locomotive is seen at London Euston on 8 May 1999 with the 18.45 to Wolverhampton.
Brian Morrison

English, Welsh & Scottish Railway

A bold step by EWS, at a time when no variation of the EWS corporate livery was expected to be allowed, was the decision to honour an important customer, British Steel, with two locomotives painted in the customer's own corporate style. The two Class 60 Co-Co diesel-electrics were painted light blue overall, with an orange lining band along the base of the bodysides. Otherwise the style was standard, apart from the presence of the British Steel badge and legend on the mid-bodysides. Now that British Steel is part of the Corus consortium, this special livery has been replaced on these locomotives by overall silver-grey, with Corus branding.

Left:
EWS pleased one of its key customers by painting Co-Co No 60006 in British Steel blue, as photographed at Warrington on 15 May 1999. The locomotive has now been repainted silver and re-branded, following British Steel's integration into the Corus group in 2000.

Below:
No 60033 shows off the new Corus livery at Toton on 24 November 2000.
Brian Morrison

Right:
Another Caledonian blue application was to ScotRail DMU No 101 692. The lining is in yellow and orange; presumably the orange is actually 'Strathclyde red'. The unit was photographed working the 07.43 from Glasgow Central to Whifflet on 31 March 1999.

Right:
Seen at Exeter on 7 December 1999, First Great Western's prototype car-carrying vehicle was painted blue and white. This was the livery of Forward Trust (now HSBC) Rail, which funded the conversion. *Colin J. Marsden*

Below:
Porterbrook added a fading blue strip to its livery when painting this demonstration Mk 3 sleeper conversion, seen at Wolverton on 17 June 1997.
Colin J. Marsden

Appendix C: Advertising Liveries

Eurostar

One Eurostar train made high-speed history by receiving an all-over yellow livery to promote the re-release of The Beatles' film *Yellow Submarine*. With the exception of the power cars, which remained unchanged, all 18 articulated carriages received full-bodyside-height plastic decals for the promotion. At least with such a livery change it is possible to remove the offending decals afterwards so that normality can return. More recent promotions have decorated a train for the musical *Notre Dame de Paris* and another for the film *102 Dalmatians*.

Left:
By using printed vinyls, even the most complex liveries can be easily applied without taking trains out of service for more than a few days. This is a detail of the 'Yellow Submarine' livery that appeared on a Eurostar train during 1999. *Bob Sweet*

Below:
Complete coverage of the sides of this Eurostar train with vinyls enabled the *Notre Dame* production at the Dominion Theatre, London, to be widely advertised. The train was at Waterloo International on 23 May 2000. *Brian Morrison*

Gatwick Express

In 1999 and 2000, some Mk 2 coaches in Gatwick Express rakes received an advertising livery promoting Continental Airlines. The lower body panels were mid-blue with the advertising material emblazoned along them. A bright red lining band separated the falcon grey from the blue. The advertising used adhesive vinyl sheets that were applied to the lower bodysides.

Connex South Central

In the summer of 2000, a group of the Connex South Central Class 319 units used on the London Victoria-Brighton fast services was given full-bodyside yellow advertising decals promoting a 'Great Day Out'.

West Anglia Great Northern

While some of the Class 313 and 315 units were operating in plain off-white livery (see Appendix B), the opportunity was taken to stick decals on the lower bodysides of a number of units to promote the WAGN off-peak fares for family trips.

Silverlink

Silverlink also applied an advertising livery to at least one Class 321 EMU used on its County services between Euston, Rugby/Northampton and Birmingham. This was liveried overall in off-white and had its advertising message scattered along the bodysides, largely below the windows but with an enormous '£7.00' making the point about a cheap fare between Birmingham and London. The illustration on page 124 shows this well.

South West Trains

Vinyls were used again for a promotion by SWT to encourage people to get out and about by train in its area. The gaudy decals were arrayed over the whole

Left:
Silverlink was publicising its £7.00 fare from London to Birmingham on unit 321 428, seen at Euston on 3 February 1999.

Below left:
The Royal British Legion is promoted with this advertising livery of SWT Class 455 unit No 5864, at Waterloo on 2 November 2000. *Brian Morrison*

Below:
For some time this Class 143 unit represented Cardiff Railways' only livery change! No 143 611 promotes the idea of going into the Valleys for a day out, against the flow of most peaktime travel. At Cardiff Central on 9 February 2000, the unit forms the 15.47 from Penarth to Rhymney.

bodysides of some Class 455 suburban four-car EMUs in 2000. More discreet was a unit decorated on behalf of The Royal British Legion for Remembrance Day 2000.

Cardiff Railways

Cardiff Railways' services bring to the Welsh capital hordes of valley folk on shopping and work journeys; to encourage city-dwellers to go and explore the valleys to provide a counter-flow of passenger journeys, the company put colourful decals on two Class 142 'Pacer' units.

General

It has to be said that, with the possible exception of the Gatwick Express Continental Airlines promotion, these advertising liveries (while undoubtedly eye-catching) exhibit a distinct lack of taste: gaudiness does not equate to beauty. There is a huge difference between the startling livery styles devised by professional stylists and the somewhat garish efforts of the advertisers to attract our attention using these special train liveries. The illustrations in this book show a selection that cannot be complete; there will certainly be many more advertising liveries on trains, and their number is likely to increase rapidly over the next few years.

Left:
In 1998 Virgin Trains had a couple of Mk 2 coaches advertising reduced off-peak fares. *Colin J. Marsden*

Left:
'...are you being taken for a ride?' asks this ScotRail Class 170 vehicle, at Edinburgh on 1 December 2000, as part of a campaign to persuade people to buy *The Herald* newspaper.

Left:
Vodafone paid for certain end cars of Heathrow Express units to promote its products, as seen on unit No 332 005, photographed at London Paddington on 13 October 2000.

Right:
A really gaudy Class 47, No 47627, sells Mars 'Celebrations' at St Pancras on 17 September 1997.
Colin J. Marsden

Appendix D: Livery Colour Definitions

Based on the response of train operators to the author's requests for information, it has been possible to glean data of colour specifications used in modern train liveries. Though not a complete record, they are listed here for their potential usefulness.

The principal specification numbers given here are as listed in BR Specification 81 (listed as BR 81/), BS381c *Specification for colours for identification, coding & special purposes*, BS4800 *Schedule of paint colours for building purposes*, or are from manufacturers' own paint identification lists, or are Pantone reference numbers used in the printing industry.

Gatwick Express

Falcon grey — BR 81/246
Silver white — BR 81/240
Warning yellow — BR 81/202 or 450; BS4800 08 E 51

Great North Eastern Railway

Midnight blue — Pantone 5395; PPG Deltron EFT-64925
GNER red — Pantone 032; PPG Deltron EFT-10327
Metallic gold — Scotchcal 3630-131 (not 'retro-reflective')
White — Scotchcal 100F-10

First Great Western

Those reference numbers beginning with 28/ are from the Railpart (former BR) catalogue. They are not strictly colour references, but may be useful.
GW green — 28/6482
Ivory — 28/5479
Silver white — 28/6151
Semi-gloss black — 28/6030
Warning yellow — 28/5316; BR 81/202 or 450
Orange warning — 28/4461

Virgin Trains

Red — BR 81/241; PPG FLT 10458
Grey — BR 81/246; PPG FLT 6758
OHLE warning orange — BR 81/500; tape/PPG FLT 10083

Midland Mainline

'Teal' green — ICI WJ87
Tangerine — RAL 2011
Silver gleam — ICI 0647

First Great Eastern

GE green — Pantone 355C
GE dark grey — Pantone 430C
GE blue — Pantone 280C
GE white — Pantone cool grey 2C
Warning yellow — BS4800 08 E 51

West Anglia Great Northern

Buttermilk — ICI XY45
Red — RAL 3020
Blue — RAL 5010

Silverlink

Cadbury's purple — ICI XW38; Pantone 2735
Bright green — ICI VI75; Pantone 376
Black — RAL 9004
White — RAL 9003
Yellow — RAL 1003
Warning yellow — BS4800 08 E 51
Orange OHLE warning — BR 81/500; tape to BS381c 557

Chiltern Railways

Red — RAL 3020
White — RAL 9016
Blue — RAL 5002
Yellow — BS4800 08 E 51
Black — RAL 9011
Light grey — RAL 7038

South West Trains

Blue (on skirt) — RAL 5010
Blue (across windows) — BS381c 105
Orange (band on blue) — RAL 2011
Orange (wave) — BS381c 368
Red — RAL 3020
Off-white — RAL 9002

Central Trains

Bright green — ICI VI75
Yellow — BR 81/202

Royal Mail

Red — Royal Mail Red
Yellow — Royal Mail Yellow
Black — BR 81/205
Dark grey — BR 81/201
Warning yellow — BR 81/202; BS4800 08 E 51
OHLE warning orange — Scotchcal 3630-44-Orange
Royal Mail logo — RM part EC:X
    (SC:X for Scottish-based units)
Royal Mail crown — RM part RCY:X
    (SCR:X for Scottish-based units)

English, Welsh & Scottish Railway

Maroon — colour matched from sample plates
    provided by Wisconsin Central Railroad
Executive dark grey — BR 81/201

Freightliner

Freightliner green — PMS 343
Freightliner yellow — PMS 116
Freightliner red — PMS 032
Orange OHLE warning — BS381c 557

NB: Colours for which no reference has been advised are omitted from this list.

In Wales & West's new 'Alphaline' livery, Class 158 Unit No 158745 leaves Ashchurch with the 1443 Birmingham New Street-Cardiff on 31 March 2000.
Bob Sweet